DISCOVERING PRAYER

Discovering Prayer

INSPIRING COMMENTARY
ON THE WEEKDAY
SHEMONEH ESREI

Ashkenaz Edition

Doniel Berger

Neshama

JERUSALEM

This publication contains words of Torah.
Please treat it with due respect.

First published 1999
ISBN 1-58330-377-4

Hebrew and English contents
© Copyright 1999 by
Doniel Berger

edited by: Aviva Rappaport

published by:
NESHAMA PRESS
POB 43193
Jerusalem, Israel

distributed by:
FELDHEIM PUBLISHERS
POB 35002, Jerusalem, Israel 91350
200 Airport Executive Park, Nanuet, N.Y. 10954

Printed in Israel

10 9 8 7 6 5 4 3 2 1

THIS EDITION IS DEDICATED IN MEMORY
OF MY DEAR GRANDPARENTS

אסתר   מאיר
בת   בן
אברהם יצחק   שרגא
א' ר"ח אלול תנש"א   י"ד סיון תשד"ם

BY THEIR LOVING CHILDREN

Mr. and Mrs. Julius Berger
Eleanor Berger, Solomon Berger
Rabbi & Mrs. Chaim Berger
Mr. & Mrs. Samuel Berger

ת . נ . צ . ב . ה .

WE REGRET THE PASSING OF MY UNCLES'
JULIUS AND SOLOMON PRIOR TO PUBLICATION.

THIS EDITION IS DEDICATED IN MEMORY
OF MY DEAR GRANDFATHER

אברהם יהושע העשיל
בן
חיים אהרון
שמיני עצרת תשל"ג

BY HIS LOVING WIFE
Channah London

AND CHILDREN
Mr. and Mrs. Jacob Cohen
Mr. & Mrs. Manuel London
Mr. & Mrs. Elliot Friend
Rabbi & Mrs. Chaim Berger

ת . נ . צ . ב . ה .

Rabbi CHAIM P. SCHEINBERG
Rosh Hayeshiva "TORAH-ORE"
and Morah Hora'ah of Kiryat Mattersdorf

הרב חיים פינחס שיינברג

ראש ישיבת »תורה-אור«

ומורה הוראה דקרית מטרסדורף

מכתב ברכה

כ״ג אייר, תשנ״ט

Reb Doniel Berger נ״י, a distinguished member of the kollel of Yeshiva Torah Ore, has provided the English speaking public with a very significant composition — a ספר called "Discovering Prayer." For many, tefillah has been under-utilized and routine.   By reading this ספר, much can be accomplished in terms of strengthening our belief and trust in Hashem, as well as our D'veikus to Hashem. The ספר opens our eyes to the importance of tefillah, the appreciation of life, the constant kindness Hashem bestows upon us, as well as the many other things חז״ל imbedded into our prayers. May the inspiring introduction and concise running commentary on each phrase of the Shemoneh Esrei provide an excellent opportunity to refresh and revitalize our devotion to Yiddishkeit and to re-think, understand, and remind ourselves about the proper goals and aspirations of life.

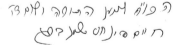

רחוב פנים מאירות 2, ירושלים, ת. ד. 6979, טל. 371513־(02), ישראל

2, Panim Meirot St., Jerusalem, P. O. B. 6 9 7 9, Tel (02)-371513, Israel

ב״ה

י״א מנחם אב תש[]ח

Rabbi Doniel Berger, shlita, a talmud chochim in his own right and son of our esteemed and dear friend, Rabbi Chaim Berger Shlita formally Rav of Kansas City, has undertaken to add additional insight into the prayer of the Shemonah Esrei, the Silent Amida. One of the great zechusim of Klal Yisrael is that we are permitted access through Tefilla thrice daily to commune with Hashem Yisbarach.

Chazal tell us that one of the reasons the Patriarchs and Matriarchs had difficulty in conceiving and having children was because Hakadosh Baruch Hu desires to hear the supplications of His righteous ones. Thus we see how important tefillah is in determining world events.

I am sure that the sefer "Discovering Prayer" will add to the global understanding and the depth of intent which one may aspire to achieve through prayer.

As a beloved Mispallel of the shul, I can personally attest and ascribe on the part of Rabbi Doniel Berger to practice that which he teaches.

May our prayers merit us so that Klal Yisrael be redeemed speedily and in our days.

המצפה לישועות השם,

The Bostoner Rebbe

מעלות האדמו״ר מבוסטון 1, ת.ד. 43033, הר נוף, ירושלים 91430
Har Nof, Jerusalem, Israel

ב״ה

[handwritten letter]

לכבוד דניאל ברגר שליט״א,

דברים שעומדים ברומו של עולם ובני אדם מזלזלין בהן as תפילה describe (Berachos 6b Rashi ibid.) חז״ל something of great significance — effecting the entire universe — that unfortunately is often taken for granted. Your ספר, the product of years of עמלות בתורה א״י will inspire multitudes of Kial Yisroel to daaven as they should. Every aspect of this sefer — its powerful new insights explaining with painstaking care every word of the Shemoneh Esrei — its captivating state-of-the-art graphics making it ideal for the traveler — its cogent explanation of the significance and impact of tefilla and its thorough review of the Halachos pertaining to daavening are all excellent. יה״ר that the tefillos that will be recited from your סידור will accelerate the גאולה שלימה.

יוסף שטרן

Contents

ANOTHER SIDDUR!?

Another Siddur!?

The above title reflects what is probably the foremost question on the reader's mind: Why another siddur?

While the siddur is the most widely published Jewish text, even its widespread daily usage fails to reveal its beauty and purpose to many of us. Several years ago, I decided to seek meaning in the most critical segment of the daily prayers — the *Shemoneh Esrei*. My research was recorded in a notebook and shared with others, who enthusiastically encouraged me to publish these insights to make them available to the broader public.

At the time, I did not think it would take seven years to complete the project. It was my family's loyal support, along with the constant encouragement of friends, that allowed me to see the project through to completion. While volumes could be (and have been) written on the subject, my goal was to create a travel-size *Shemoneh Esrei* which offers briefly expressed yet profound glimpses into the meaning of the prayer.

To properly gain from this siddur, it is recommended that you first read and familiarize yourself with the material before using it while praying. It is my sincere hope that *Discovering Prayer* will assist you in rediscovering the *Shemoneh Esrei* and inspire you to pray with a deeper consciousness of the words you are saying. Through our efforts, may we all merit to see and experience the coming of the *Mashiach*, speedily in our days. Amen.

Doniel Dov Berger
Kiryat Sefer
Eretz Yisrael / Tishrei, 5760 (99)

Acknowledgments

I wish to thank and express my deepest gratitude to the following:

- First and foremost, I thank Hashem for giving me the ability and the opportunity to write, as well as publish, this siddur.

- The Rosh HaYeshiva, Hagaon Harav Chaim Pinchas Scheinberg *shlita*, for teaching me and advising me on all things, big and small.

- Rabbi Eliezer Parkoff for allowing me the use of Yeshiva Shaare Chaim's computer and printer.

- Harav Chaim Dov Altusky, Rabbi Yisroel Berl, Rabbi Yissachor Heller, Rabbi Dovid Krohn, Rabbi Yosef Krohn, Rabbi Moshe Lewis, Rabbi Eliezer Parkoff, Rabbi Tzvi Pincus, Rabbi Yaakov Pinsky, and Rabbi Zvi Zobin, for proofreading sections of the original manuscript.

- Rabbi Menachem Roodman for proofreading the first version.

- Rabbi Yisroel Altusky, Rabbi Shia Chaitovsky, Rabbi Mordechai Dolinsky, Maran HaMashgiach Harav Zeidel Epstein *shlita*, Rabbi Moshe Finkelstein, Harav Simcha Scheinberg, Harav Yosef Stern, as well as the previously mentioned *Rabbonim*, for providing me with the knowledge that went into producing this siddur.

- R' Dovid Ballon, R' Efraim Krohn and R' Dovid Vatch for helping me write the first draft.

- R' and Mrs. Aron Vinitsky and R' Yaakov Yisroel Babad for their advice.

- R' Yaakov Feldheim for time and advice in "How to Publish a Book."

- Mrs. Aviva Rappaport for her superb editing and general enhancement of the text.

- R' Akiva Atwood for doing such a terrific job with the elaborate layout.

- D. Liff for the finishing touches of the interior.

- My parents, Rabbi and Mrs. Chaim Berger, and my wife's parents, Mr. and Mrs. Naftoli Coleman, for their constant understanding and support. May they always receive *nachas* from their children.

- My brother, Rabbi Yosef Shraga Berger, for editing the *Guidelines* section, and for all his help over the years.

- My family for dedicating this inaugural edition in loving memory of my grandparents. May this siddur be a merit for them.

- Mrs. Devorah Rhein for the painstaking proofreading.

- And a very special thanks to my wife, Sharon, for being an *Aishes Chayil*, for her patience, advice, and assistance.

About this siddur

- This siddur presents a concise, meaningful commentary. It should be kept in mind that many laws concerning the *Shemoneh Esrei*, such as when and how to bow, are not presented here. The preparation of a more detailed, expanded edition for beginners is currently underway.

- The English translation is printed in bold text, followed by the commentary.

- I have reversed the traditional linear layout by writing the translation to the right of the Hebrew text. I did so because it is my opinion that this creates a better relationship between the Hebrew words and the commentary, since in this layout the two are closer together.

- Where a common alternative text exists, it has been added in brackets, with the following three exceptions:

1. In the ninth blessing of בָּרֵךְ עָלֵינוּ — **Bless on our behalf** (page 63), the alternative text is inserted on the next line in gray.

2. The paragraph of שָׁלוֹם רָב — **Abundant peace**, (page 105), which is said during *Ma'ariv* and usually during *Minchah*, is enclosed by a frame.

3. In the nineteenth blessing of שִׂים שָׁלוֹם — **Place peace** (page 106), the alternative text is inserted on the previous line in gray (it might be helpful to bracket the version you do not use).

- There are five times when the alternative text is seasonal, in which case both versions are printed side by side. Instructions are given at each of these locations explaining when each version is to be said (page 47, 48, 63, 68, 112).

- In a situation where there is an alternative text and you said the wrong one, or are in doubt, a box on the side directs you to a section in the back explaining how to proceed.

- All the prayers recited only on special occasions have been grayed to minimize distraction in the flow when they are not being said.

- Large, clear reminders have been inserted stating where and when the prayers recited on special occasions are to be added.

- Two optional prayers have been inserted (page 60 and 109); these are grayed and enclosed in a frame.

- When the Shemoneh Esrei is repeated out loud by the chazzan, we answer אָמֵן at the completion of each blessing. When we answer Amen, we are voicing our affirmation of the blessing just recited. In this siddur, each Amen is followed by a brief explanation of the specific confirmation.

- *Minchah* and *Ma'ariv* appear at the end of this siddur, and can be easily accessed by opening from the back cover.

Our prayers are multi-faced and contain many meanings. The commentary presented here has been chosen for its inspirational value and is by no means the only possible interpretation of the text. All efforts have been made to maintain clarity and eliminate errors, yet human fallibility being what it is, if you do have any comments or questions please forward them to Neshama Press.

PRAYER
REASSESSED

Prayer Reassessed

Prayer has always been a special part of human existence. Sadly though, prayer has become like a pauper in rags begging for a handout. Most people pass right by, too busy to take any notice. Some will pause, somewhat reluctantly, long enough to drag a few coins from their pockets. Very few will actually stop and show a true sense of concern for the unfortunate individual.

What prevents us from praying sincerely, from the heart? What compels so many of us to arrive late for prayers, mumble our way through, and leave early? What causes us to neglect prayer and inadvertently treat it with some degree of disrespect?

The answer: Lack of awareness of prayer's impact on the world.

Prayer is a powerful entity that is compared to a sword.[1] Just as a soldier would not dream of going out to battle without his weapon, so too we cannot survive the battleground of life without our weapon — prayer. Prayer is a weapon more powerful than a multi-target ballistic missile, more accurate than the most sophisticated guidance system. Prayer has the ability to make the sun stand still and even to resurrect the dead. Prayer can prevent or diminish suffering. No matter how severe the sin, sincere prayer can open the gates of repentance. Prayer gives us the opportunity to become close to Hashem. Its meaning is deeper than even the greatest human intellect can fathom.

Shimon HaTzaddik taught,[2] "Three things serve as the foundation of existence, "Torah, *Avodah*, and acts of lovingkindness." Each of these activities provides essential nourishment and sustenance for the entire universe, without which the world we live in would cease to exist. Any deficiency or weakness in these three pillars of existence is immediately felt in the entire creation. The second of the three, *Avodah*, refers to the priestly service conducted in the *Beis Hamikdash*.[3] When the destruction of the *Beis Hamikdash* interrupted the daily offerings, they were replaced by the "offerings of our lips"[4] — prayer.[5] Our prayers, then, are a vital ingredient in keeping the world going!

But...how does prayer work? What makes it such a powerful force?

Prayer influences our lives and the world in many different ways. It has the power to improve our character by imbuing us with: belief and trust in Hashem; enhanced perception and appreciation of His endless wonders; feelings of gratitude to our Creator, leading to a desire to praise and thank Him; adoration of the Torah He gave us and a yearning to live by it; and a driving desire to be close to and serve Him to the maximum of our physical and mental capacities. It is for this very reason — for our own personal development — that prayer was fixed as a daily obligation.

Belief and trust

Belief and trust in Hashem are two essential basics of Judaism. We want to work at developing a constant awareness that Hashem single-handedly reigns over the entire universe, is the Source of all powers and abilities, and controls every aspect of existence. To believe in Hashem is to believe that no occurrence is just "coincidence" or "an accident." To believe in Hashem is to believe that there is no task beyond His ability to accomplish.

If someone were to ask us, "Do you believe in God?" our answer would be an emphatic "Yes." Yet why is it that only after all other sources of possible assistance are exhausted do we say, "All we can do now is pray"? Why is it that only when something terrible befalls us do we suddenly cry out to heaven? Why should Hashem be the *last* thing on our minds instead of the *first*?

Let us listen and learn from King David, the Psalmist of Israel:

> *I raise my eyes to the mountains — from where will my help come? My help is from Hashem, Maker of heaven and earth. He will not let your foot stumble; your Guardian will not slumber. Behold, the Guardian of Israel neither slumbers nor sleeps. Hashem is your guardian; Hashem is your shadow at your right hand. The sun will not harm you by day, nor the moon by night. Hashem will guard you from all evil; He will guard your soul. Hashem will guard your departure and your arrival, from now and forever.*[6]

Our **first** instinct should always be to call out to our Father in heaven for assistance.

Prayer also reminds us that the foremost solution and ultimate solution to all difficulties lies with Hashem. Although we profess belief in Hashem, the real proof of our belief is whether we have complete trust in Him in *every* aspect of our lives. As King David said so wisely in *Tehillim*:

> *It is better to take refuge in Hashem than to place trust in a human being. It is better to take refuge in Hashem than to trust in mortal benefactors.*[7]

> *Do not place your trust in noble men, in mortals who have no ability to save.*[8]

Faced with challenge, King David understood with absolute clarity that his salvation could only come from Hashem. The Prophets in their writings echoed this same thought, as have our sages from generation to generation. Even though we are planted in the physical world, we must reach for the heavens. Although we interact with our fellow humans, our hearts and souls depend entirely on Hashem for protection and deliverance.

Trusting in Hashem leaves all options open. To trust in Hashem means never giving up hope, no matter how grim the situation may appear. The more we are prepared to rely solely on Hashem, the greater He reciprocates assistance. This is the meaning of the verse "Hashem is your shadow at your right hand" — if you reveal your finger outwards, it creates a shadow of a finger; if your whole hand, then a shadow of a whole hand. So too, if we hold back on our trust, if we are only prepared to rely upon Hashem half-heartedly, then He responds with assistance in moderation. Just think of how things would be if we were willing to totally dedicate ourselves to Hashem!

On the other hand, if we become obsessed with a life totally void of our Creator, can we honestly blame Him for our lack of sincerity? He stretches out His hand to redeem us from our misery, yet we just stare blankly. When Hashem knocked, we never answered; now that we need Him, He is nowhere to be found. Once again, King David leads us on the proper path:

> *Those knowing Your Name will trust in You, for You have not forsaken those who seek You, Hashem.*[9]

We need to pour out our hearts to the All Merciful and say, "Master of the universe! I acknowledge that **You** are our true salvation." Daily prayer is a constant reminder to trust in Hashem and to always call upon Him for help.

Prayer offers not only salvation, but protection as well.

When our forefather, Yitzchak, said, "The voice is the voice of Yaakov, but the hands are the hands of Eisav,"[10] he revealed to the descendants of Yaakov — the Jewish people — a crucial lesson for survival: it is Yaakov's *voice* that will protect him from the hateful *hands* of his adversaries.[11] When we "voice" our recognition of the Alm-ghty through supplication (in addition to the many mitzvos we can perform with our mouth), we earn heavenly protection.

Enhanced perception and appreciation

Hashem endlessly dedicates Himself to our welfare. In return, He asks that we show our appreciation by devoting ourselves to: serve Him, honor Him, thank Him, and love Him with all our heart, all our soul, and all our possessions. To take the priceless gift of life and focus it on fulfilling our own desires would be ingratitude, and would express an extremely selfish lack of appreciation.

> Just being alive is reason enough to endlessly
> thank our Creator!

Life is the most basic as well as the most important gift we have been given, yet we tend to take it for granted. Most of us rarely reflect on our lives. Out of habit, we assume upon retiring at night that we will wake up. Most likely, we have even planned the coming day. In reality, though, each night our soul ascends to Heaven for judgment.[12] The outcome of this call to justice will decide whether or not the soul will be returned to the body below. When Hashem, Who is never short of giving us a second chance, mercifully allows our souls to return to our bodies upon awakening, He has chosen to allow us a renewal of life — with the assumption that we will make better use of our brief presence in this world.

Feeling and expressing gratitude

Feeling and expressing gratitude for any kindness received is such an important character trait. For this reason, parents begin teaching it to their children from their earliest years. It is a quality that needs to become part of our inner being so that it will be constantly reflected in all our social interactions.

Hashem, too, wanted humanity to learn this important lesson at an early age, as we see from the narrative of Noach.

We are told that Noach was so righteous that Hashem chose him to be the source of mankind's regeneration after the Flood. At the same time, we learn that he was heavily burdened with caring for all the animals in the ark. The round-the-clock responsibility of feeding the only remaining animals on land[13] left Noach without even a minute for himself. How could the Merciful One have seemingly oppressed this righteous man with such an excruciatingly demanding task?

The answer is that it was very clear to Hashem that if mankind was going to change from its previous corrupt ways, it would have to learn the importance of gratitude. The One Above wanted the few remaining people who would repopulate the world to have a deep understanding of what He Himself does. The constant responsibility for the animals' survival taught Noach and his family to appreciate Hashem's constant care-taking of all creation.

Perhaps if we would realize that death is an inescapable fact of life it would be easier for us to truly appreciate and cherish every second of our lives. Before we are even born, it has already been decided when each of us will die (although it is possible to merit an extension). If a doctor were to tell someone that he has only six more months to live, he would fervently try to make the most of those precious six months. But what if the doctor were to tell that same person that he is critically ill, yet it is uncertain how much time he has left, that it might be many years, or it might only be a few days? Wouldn't any logically thinking person try to make each day meaningful? Wouldn't he want each day to be as productive as possible?

We are in exactly the same situation. Since we do not know when we will die, every second of life is nothing less than a precious gift. For every breath of air we take, for every beat of our heart, should we not be busy thanking Hashem? These moving words from the Shabbos morning prayers eloquently express this thought:

> *Were our mouths as full of song as the sea, and our tongues as full of joyous song as its multitude of waves, and our lips as full of praise as the expanse of the heavens, and our eyes as radiant as the sun and the moon, and our hands as outspread as eagles of the sky, and our feet as swift as hinds — we still could not thank You enough, Hashem, our God, and the God of our forefathers.*[14]

Prayer reminds us to appreciate every second of life.

With prayer, we come to realize and understand the significance of gratitude to our Creator. Complaining that prayer services are too long (and therefore wasteful of time which could better be used for "more important" things) is like saying, "I do not need to express any gratitude"!

Adoration of the Torah

Mankind continues to struggle with the concept of creating a perfect society free from social disorder. Due to lack of clear-cut universally accepted guidelines, people have relied mainly on individual conscience to determine what is morally correct and what is not. Opinions differ widely, since no two people think the same, inevitably leading to conflict, with each person defending what is, in his opinion, morally just.

Hashem, Who is All Knowing, foresaw the problems that would plague our societies and fashioned the Torah on the very principles which can prevent them. The Torah — the Master Plan for existence, is not only the blueprint for creation, but also the single guideline for a perfect society and continued existence. Its superb guidance sets everything in its place and proper time, in exact measure. Nothing is superfluous.[15] This pedagogue of proper conduct and justice was offered to every people on earth, yet each one in turn rejected it, claiming that its guidelines conflicted with their lifestyle. Only the Jewish people were willing to embrace the Torah in its entirety. The acceptance ceremony was the revelation at Mount Sinai, fulfilling the Divine Master Plan for Creation.

Mark Twain once wrote[16] that he was puzzled by the immortality of the Jewish people. How could it be, he asked, that a nation which had been continually subjugated to exile and death survived throughout the millennia while those who had conquered it no longer even existed. There is only one answer: It is the Torah which sustains the Jewish people. When they proclaimed, "We will do and we will listen," they bonded themselves to the eternal Torah and eternally guaranteed their destiny as the Chosen Nation of Hashem, His prize possession.

The great sage Hillel summarized the entire Torah in one brief sentence: "Love your fellow man as yourself." He was teaching us that the purpose of the commandments is to refine our character and increase our sensitivity to all that is just and morally correct.[17] When we live by the statutes of the Torah, we create a fine-tuned and unified society, which generates a harmony that spreads throughout the universe.

Prayer teaches us to cherish and respect the priceless and precious gift of Torah.

Making the most out of life

Even if we realize we could do more, we hesitate before accepting the need to change our habits. We may rationalize, "I keep Shabbos, I keep kosher, give to charity, celebrate the holidays, perform whatever mitzvos come my way, and pray daily — isn't that enough?"

The answer is: No!

It is a common misconception to think that it's possible to maintain a status quo spiritually. In reality, the spiritual world parallels the physical. Just as all physical life at any given second is either growing or decaying, so too a person cannot stand still spiritually. If we are not growing, we are decaying.

When Rabbi Shimon Schwab *ztz"l*, the previous leader of German Jewry in New York, was a young man, he traveled from Germany to Lithuania to study in the great European yeshivos of Telshe and Mir. At the time, Rabbi Schwab was a student already well-versed in Torah, having been raised in a community strengthened by the powerful teachings of Rabbi Samson Rafael Hirsch. Yet it was in Lithuania that he became inspired by a concept that would change his life. There he was introduced to the term "*shteig*", a Yiddish expression for spiritual growth.[18] To *shteig* is to constantly say to oneself, "I am unsatisfied with my spiritual level. I want to grow spiritually and strengthen my connection to Hashem. I want to improve my character, fulfill mitzvos with greater fervor, seek ways to help my fellow man, and pray with all my heart."

Let us make it our goal to *shteig*, to develop a yearning to pray and to feel an overwhelming joy for the opportunity we have been given to speak directly to Hashem. An easy way to improve in this area is to ask ourselves: "How does prayer play a part in my life? Can it help me succeed? Can prayer give me a better understanding of my Creator and the extent of the role He plays in my life, the role I play in the lives of others, and the role they play in mine?"

Often people think, "Maybe I'm not capable of doing more." Yet we know that Hashem, Who is All-knowing and very much aware of our limitations, only asks of us what we are capable of doing. This means that true, heartfelt prayer is within our reach.

There are others who say, "Who says Hashem will listen?" This is a mistake, for every prayer is heard. Do not even think for a second that Hashem will not listen, for He always sees our efforts, knows our thoughts, and hears our words. This does not mean, though, that our requests will automatically be granted, since only the One Who is All-knowing can perceive what is truly best for us.

Prayer is called the "service of the heart."[19] Serving Hashem with all our heart requires that we understand and take to heart the significance of the words that pass our lips and ascend to heaven. It demands a belief in the very words we utter and in the endless effects they have. It is only due to our lack of understanding that praying has become so habitual that often we merely mumble the words in haste.

More than two thousand years ago, the one hundred and twenty scholars of the Great Assembly, amongst them prophets, instituted the *Shemoneh Esrei* to be the center of every daily prayer session. If we delve into the *Shemoneh Esrei*, searching for insight and understanding, it can reveal to us fundamental ideas and values which will strengthen our faith. It will increase our understanding of Hashem, the world around us, and ourselves.

As we step forward at the opening of the *Shemoneh Esrei*, each of us stands alone in the presence of Hashem, leaving behind the burdens of everyday life. Our Father in Heaven gives each of us His undivided attention and awaits our requests. He grants us a special opportunity to talk directly to Him, one to One (so to speak).

Make it worthwhile. Open your heart to Hashem, and He will open His heart to you.

אֲדֹנָי שְׂפָתַי תִּפְתָּח וּפִי יַגִּיד תְּהִלָּתֶךָ

"My Master, open my lips so my mouth may pronounce Your praise."[20]

---

1. *Targum* on *Bereishis* 48:22.

2. *Pirkei Avos* 1:2.

3. ibid. Rashi; *Rabbeinu Yonah*.

4. *Hoshea* 14:3.

5. *Pirkei Avos* 1:2, *Rabbeinu Yonah*; *Ta'anis* 27b, *Yoma* 86a.

6. *Tehillim* 121.

7. *Tehillim* 118:8-9.

8. *Tehillim* 146:3.

9. *Tehillim* 9:11.

10. *Bereishis* 27:22.

11. ibid. *Bereishis Rabbah*.

12. *Midrash Tanchuma Hayashan* (*Mishpatim*:9).

13. Animals that live in the sea were not included in the decree of annihilation.

14. תפילת נשמת

15. *Pathways*, Rabbi Shlomo Wolbe (Israel: Feldheim Publishers, 1983), page 28.

16. *An Essay Concerning the Jews*, (Harper's Magazine, 1899).

17. *Masterplan*, Aryeh Carmel (Israel: Jerusalem Academy Publications, 1991) page 121.

18. *Selected Writings*, Rav Shimon Schwab (Lakewood, NJ: C.I.S. Publications, 1988).

19. *Ta'anis* 2a.

20. *Tehillim* 51:7.

SAYING IT RIGHT!

Saying it right

Two commonly mispronounced words in prayer are ה׳ and בָּרוּךְ.

ה׳ is often incorrectly pronounced AH-DEH-NAI, AH-DEE-NAI, AH-DOE-NAI, AH-DEH-NOY, or AH-DEE-NOY. The correct pronunciation is **AH-DOE-NOY** with the accent on the last syllable.

בָּרוּךְ is often mistakenly pronounced B'RUKH or B'ROOKH. The correct pronunciation is BAH-RUKH with the accent on the last syllable.

Emphasis is always on the last syllable of a word, unless an earlier syllable is marked with a vertical line (מֶתֶג) underneath the letter. For example:

אָבִינוּ

In that case, the syllable which is marked should be accented instead.

Where appropriate, a vocal *shv'a* (שְׁוָא נָע) has been marked in the text. Letters to be emphasized have been marked with a circle above them. For example:

קָדֹשׁ

Throughout the text, the word אַתָּה, "You" (Hashem) and the suffix נוּ, the collective "we" or "us," have been made bold and larger in size. The emphasis on the word אַתָּה serves as a reminder that we are standing before Hashem. Emphasis on the plural suffix נוּ serves to stress that we pray for *everyone's* needs.

THE
SHEMONEH
ESREI

Before Minchah add the following two lines

כִּי שֵׁם יהוה אֶקְרָא **When I call out the name of the Master of the Universe Who was, is, and always will be,**[1]

הָבוּ גֹדֶל לֵאלֹהֵינוּ **assign greatness to our God, Source of all powers and abilities.**[2]

We all agree that speech plays a major role in everyday life. Hashem gave us the power of speech to use for beneficial and productive purposes. Unfortunately, we often take this gift for granted, abusing our power of speech in meaningless or even damaging ways. We have sometimes spoken negatively, making derogatory statements about others. Our gossip, ridicule, and backbiting have caused others embarrassment. We have at times lied, cursed, used unclean language, revealed secrets and provoked animosity. How can we possibly stand before Hashem and speak to Him after using our mouth for such disgraceful things? We therefore preface our prayers with this request:

אֲדֹנָי שְׂפָתַי תִּפְתָּח **My Master,**[3] **open my lips,**

I know that I have abused my power of speech and sincerely wish to change my ways. Therefore, Hashem, Master of the Universe, give me the strength to open my lips, the guardians of speech,

וּפִי יַגִּיד תְּהִלָּתֶךָ **so that my mouth may pronounce Your praise.**

So that I may use Your gift of speech for good purposes.[4]

‎ﭏ 1: The Patriarchs ‎ﭏﭏ

בָּרוּךְ אַתָּה **Blessed are You**[1]

We stand before Hashem, talking directly to Him,[2] and He in return gives us His personal attention. He hears everything we say and knows all our thoughts.

יהוה **Master of the Universe, Who was, is, and always will be,**

He existed before creation, exists now, and will continue to exist for eternity.

אֱלֹהֵינוּ **our God, Source of all powers and abilities,**

Divine Providence guides everything. Nothing is coincidental or accidental. No matter who we are or where we are, Hashem constantly provides us with all our needs.

וֵאלֹהֵי אֲבוֹתֵינוּ **and God of our Forefathers,**

Our Forefathers served Hashem according to their exalted level of understanding their Creator. We, who lack their insight, cannot possibly serve Him as they did. We should not feel discouraged though, since Hashem only obligates each of us to understand and serve Him to the limits of our own capacities (**our God**). Still, we are to remember that there is far, far more to understand (**and God of our Forefathers**).[3]

אֱלֹהֵי אַבְרָהָם   **The God of Avraham,**

Each of our Forefathers excelled in and mastered an attribute, and therefore each deserves to be mentioned separately.[4] Avraham recognized the attribute of *Chesed*, lovingkindness, in Hashem.[5] This led him to excel in and personify lovingkindness.

אֱלֹהֵי יִצְחָק   **the God of Yitzchak,**

Yitzchak recognized the attribute of *G'vurah*, power, in Hashem.[6] This led him to excel in and personify awe of heaven and fear of sin.

וֵאלֹהֵי יַעֲקֹב   **and the God of Yaakov;**

Yaakov recognized the attribute of *Emes*, truth, a synthesis of lovingkindness and power, in Hashem.[7] This led him to excel in and personify truth and trust.

הָאֵל   **the Almighty,**

The scope of Hashem's powers is unlimited.[8] His justice is supreme and unquestionable.

הַגָּדוֹל   **the Greatest,**

Not only is Hashem great beyond everything in the physical realm, He is great beyond anything in the spiritual realm.[9] Hashem is not limited to time or space.

הַגִּבּוֹר   **the Most Powerful,**

In the most minute fraction of a second, Hashem can eliminate the entire world and create another in its place. There is nothing beyond His capabilities.

וְהַנּוֹרָא **the Awe-inspiring,**

Hashem effects ultimate fear. His decrees are inescapable, and His wrath is impossible to withstand.[10]

אֵל עֶלְיוֹן **Supreme Almighty**

Hashem's rule is above and beyond everything.[11] His rule lacks nothing and lacks no one. Hashem is the Supreme Being, beyond us[12] in all dimensions.

גּוֹמֵל חֲסָדִים טוֹבִים **Who bestows good kindness,**

When a human being does an act of kindness it is impossible to know whether or not the kindness was truly beneficial, for we cannot see into the future. It is possible that the act of kindness was not only not helpful, but that it was even detrimental. Hashem's kindness, though, is *always* beneficial to its recipient and is therefore always "good" kindness.[13]

וְקוֹנֵה הַכֹּל **and possesses everything,**

Hashem created and creates everything in the world and owns everything in the world. Everything we have is only on loan from Hashem.

וְזוֹכֵר חַסְדֵּי אָבוֹת **and Who remembers the great deeds of the Forefathers,**

וּמֵבִיא גוֹאֵל **and brings a redeemer**

לִבְנֵי בְנֵיהֶם **to their children's children**

You, Hashem, will bring the Final Redemption, and if we do not merit to

have it brought in our own right,
remember the great deeds of the
Forefathers and Your promise to them,
and bring the Redemption to us — their
descendants.[14]

לְמַעַן שְׁמוֹ **for the sake of His Name**

And if even the merit of the Forefathers
is not enough to bring the Redemption,
then do it for the sake of Your Name.[15] All
the nations of the world mock us, saying,
"Look at this nation called Yisrael. They
claim to be the Chosen People, the
greatest nation ever, the children of God,
yet they are a powerless nation spread
thin all over the world, easy prey,
vulnerable to annihilation. Their claims
mean nothing." This statement is a
disgrace and a desecration of Your great
Name, so redeem us for the sake of the
sanctity of Your Name.[16]

בְּאַהֲבָה **with love.**

Even if the Redemption is brought
about neither in our merit nor in the merit
of our Forefathers, let it not be fulfilled in
disappointment, but with love.[17]

The following is added between Rosh Hashanah and Yom Kippur

זָכְרֵנוּ לְחַיִּים **Remember us for life,**

The time of judgment has arrived and
there is no guarantee that we will merit
the right to continue to live. Knowing that

it might be decided in the Heavenly Court not to extend our lives, we ask Hashem to have mercy and allow us to live.

מֶלֶךְ חָפֵץ בַּחַיִּים **King, Who desires life,**

Hashem does not desire that we die, but rather that we repent from our corrupt ways[18] and exalt His Name by following in His ways and fulfilling His commandments.

Forgot to say this? See page 132

וְכָתְבֵנוּ **and inscribe us**

בְּסֵפֶר הַחַיִּים **in the Book of Life**

לְמַעַנְךָ אֱלֹהִים חַיִּים **for Your sake, God of life.**

Only if we live can we possibly serve You, Hashem, and proclaim Your greatness by fulfilling Your commandments.[19]

Hashem implanted within us a good inclination and an evil one. The evil inclination is constantly trying to prevent us from fulfilling Hashem's will that we follow the precepts of the Torah. It is Hashem's desire that our good inclination overpower our evil inclination so that we can succeed in earning a place in the World to Come.

מֶלֶךְ **King**

Ruler over all.[20]

עוֹזֵר **Helper**

When we become ensnared by the evil inclination, You help us overcome it.[21]

וּמוֹשִׁיעַ **Savior**

And when we have fallen defenseless against our evil inclination, You come and save us.[22]

וּמָגֵן **and Shielder.**

You also shield us from falling prey to our evil inclination in the future.[23]

בָּרוּךְ אַתָּה **Blessed are You,**

יהוה **Master of the Universe, Who was, is, and always will be,**

מָגֵן אַבְרָהָם **Shield of Avraham.**

Avraham revealed to the world the basis of Judaism: that existence has a planned purpose, solely created and controlled by Hashem. Just as You, Hashem, protected Avraham, the founder of the Jewish faith, through all his trials and tribulations, so too, protect us,[24] those who continue to maintain this faith.

Amen: *It is true, and I believe with complete faith,*[25] *that Hashem Who protected Avraham, will protect us as well.*[26]

‮cs‬ 2: God's Mightiness ‮so‬

אַתָּה   **You**

(We must remember that we are standing before Hashem, speaking directly to Him)

גִּבּוֹר לְעוֹלָם   **are eternally powerful,**

אֲדֹנָי   **Master of the Universe,**

Your power never weakens.[1] Your rule over the world is permanent and continuous.[2]

Hashem is not like us, for we often use our strengths (גְבוּרָה) and abilities to further our own interests, to show that we are better, stronger, greater or more important than others, and to belittle, disgrace, and harm our fellow man. Hashem, though, uses His power to help others in unlimited ways:

מְחַיֶּה מֵתִים אַתָּה   **You are the Resurrector of the dead,**

Hashem, Himself, in the future will personally[3] restore to life all those meriting the right to resurrection, just as He revives new life in us every day when we awaken.

רַב לְהוֹשִׁיעַ   **abundant to save.**

Hashem extends this right to everyone. Anyone and everyone can merit this resurrection. Hashem's acts of rejuvenation are multi-faceted, as the following passages explain.

During the rainy season (See page 139)

מַשִׁיב הָרוּחַ וּמוֹרִיד הַגֶּשֶׁם **Causer of the wind to blow and the rain to fall,**

Wind is an important element in many aspects of life, from facilitating plant reproduction to bringing the rains necessary to supply us with food and water, which in return enable us to exist.

In Eretz Yisrael during the dry season (See page 139)

מוֹרִיד הַטָּל **Causer of the dew to fall,**

Dew plays an essential role in plant growth, especially in dry climates and during the dry season

Made a mistake? See page 139

מְכַלְכֵּל חַיִּים בְּחֶסֶד **Sustainer of the living with lovingkindness,**

Hashem continues to sustain us, attending to our constant needs, even though we may not be deserving of being kept alive.[4] Life was created for the sole purpose of serving Hashem. If we fail to serve Him as we should, we pray that He will allow us to live anyway, as a kindness.

מְחַיֶּה מֵתִים **Resurrector of the dead**

בְּרַחֲמִים רַבִּים **with abundant mercy,**

There are three ascending levels of Hashem's goodness: טוֹב - goodness, חֵן - graciousness, and רַחֲמִים - mercy. Only through Hashem's mercy in great abundance will the fortunate be resurrected for eternal life in the next world.[5] After the body is revived, it will be healed of any blemish or disability it suffered in this world.[6]

סוֹמֵךְ נוֹפְלִים — Supporter of the fallen

Throughout our history, during times of oppression and degradation, trial and tribulation, Hashem has supported us, His children, helping us to survive and rebound, never allowing us to be totally annihilated.

וְרוֹפֵא חוֹלִים — and Healer of the sick

The healing ability of doctors and medicines comes entirely from Hashem.[7] There is no illness Hashem cannot heal.[8]

וּמַתִּיר אֲסוּרִים — and Releaser of the imprisoned,

Sometimes we find ourselves faced with difficulty, which often leaves us imprisoned by despair, worry, or confusion. If we turn to Hashem[9] with our problems, He sends us the solution or gives us the ability to remedy them. We then feel as if our life has been renewed.

וּמְקַיֵּם אֱמוּנָתוֹ לִישֵׁנֵי עָפָר — and maintains His faithfulness to those who sleep in dust.

Those who reach true righteousness do not decay and disintegrate in the ground after death, but rather "sleep in the dust" totally intact, awaiting resurrection. Our righteous Forefathers sleep in the dust, waiting for Hashem to bring the Final Redemption, fulfilling His promise to raise us up above all other nations.[10]

מִי כָמְוֹךָ **Who is like You,**

בַּעַל גְּבוּרוֹת **Master of all powers,**

Now that we have a better understanding of Who Hashem is, we proclaim: Who is as marvelous as You, Hashem, Master of boundless powers and unlimited abilities!

וּמִי דוֹמֶה לָּךְ **and who compares to You,**

What earthly object or man-made pseudo-god could possibly compare to You!

מֶלֶךְ מֵמִית וּמְחַיֶּה **King Who causes death and maintains life**

Hashem alone reigns over all life and death. Nothing is created, exists, or ceases to be unless Hashem wills it.[11]

וּמַצְמִיחַ יְשׁוּעָה **and causes salvation to sprout forth.**

Hashem knows that if the Final Redemption and everything it entails were to occur all at once, we would not be able to endure it. Hashem therefore brings about the Final Redemption in an extended, slowly developing process,[12] like the growth of a tiny sprout into a gigantic tree.

The following is added between Rosh Hashanah and Yom Kippur

מִי כָמְוֹךָ **Who is like You,**

אַב הָרַחֲמִים **merciful Father**

You are like a compassionate father who is merciful to his child when the child does wrong and regrets it.[13]

זוֹכֵר יְצוּרָיו **Who remembers His creatures**
לְחַיִּים בְּרַחֲמִים **for life, in His mercy.**

Forgot
to say
this?
See page
133

If, because of our wrongdoing, we cannot rightly ask for mercy as Hashem's children, we therefore humble ourselves, calling ourselves "creatures," and plead, "Even if we are not worthy of life, inscribe us in the Book of Life anyway, since You are merciful."[14]

וְנֶאֱמָן אַתָּה **And You are trusted**
לְהַחֲיוֹת מֵתִים **to restore life to the dead.**

We say upon awakening each morning, "I give thanks to You, living and eternal King, for returning my soul within me with mercy..." Just as we have complete faith in Hashem that He will restore our souls within us each morning, so too we have complete faith in Him that He will one day resurrect the dead,[15] even though we have never seen such a thing.

בָּרוּךְ אַתָּה **Blessed are You,**

יהוה **Master of the Universe, Who was, is, and always will be,**

מְחַיֵּה הַמֵּתִים **Resurrector of the Dead.**

You, Hashem, perform acts of reviving new life every day, and will one day resurrect the dead.[16]

Amen: *It is true, and I believe with complete faith, that You will one day resurrect the dead.*[17]

❧ 3: Holiness of God's Name ☙

Kedushah

נְקַדֵּשׁ אֶת **We will sanctify**

שִׁמְךָ בָּעוֹלָם **Your Name in the world**

By carrying out the mitzvos of the Torah, we draw more and more of Hashem's holiness upon ourselves and the world.

כְּשֵׁם **just as**

שֶׁמַּקְדִּישִׁים אוֹתוֹ **they sanctify it**

Just as the angels sanctify it.

בִּשְׁמֵי מָרוֹם **in the high heavens,**

כַּכָּתוּב עַל יַד נְבִיאֶךָ **as it is written by the hand of Your prophet,**[1]

וְקָרָא זֶה אֶל זֶה וְאָמַר **"And one angel called unto the other and declared:**

קָדוֹשׁ **Holy!**

Hashem is the ultimate holiness in the spiritual world.[2]

קָדוֹשׁ **Holy!**

Hashem is the ultimate holiness in the physical world.

קָדוֹשׁ **Holy!**

Hashem is the ultimate holiness forever and for all eternity. Hashem is beyond the limits of life, space, and time.

יהוה is the Master of the Universe, Who was, is, and always will be,

צְבָאוֹת Master of heavenly legions;

מְלֹא כָל הָאָרֶץ כְּבוֹדוֹ the whole world is filled with His glory."

We and the unique and fascinating world around us glorify the greatness of Hashem.[3]

לְעֻמָּתָם בָּרוּךְ יֹאמֵרוּ Those facing them declare, "Bless!"

בָּרוּךְ כְּבוֹד "Bless the glory

יהוה of the Master of the Universe, Who was, is, and always will be,

מִמְּקוֹמוֹ from His place."[4]

"From His place," since even the holiest of angels does not know exactly where Hashem presides.[5]

וּבְדִבְרֵי קָדְשְׁךָ And in Your Holy Writings

כָּתוּב לֵאמֹר it is written, saying

יִמְלֹךְ יהוה לְעוֹלָם "The Master of the Universe, Who was, is, and always will be, will reign forever,

אֱלֹהַיִךְ צִיּוֹן your God, Source of all powers and abilities, Zion,

לְדֹר וָדֹר from generation to generation;

הַלְלוּיָהּ praise God."[6]

לְדוֹר וָדוֹר From generation to generation

נַגִּיד גָּדְלֶךָ we will tell of Your greatness

וּלְנֵצַח נְצָחִים and for infinite eternities

קְדֻשָּׁתְךָ נַקְדִּישׁ we will sanctify Your holiness,

by fulfilling Your will and dedicating every aspect of our lives to You.[7]

וְשִׁבְחֲךָ אֱלֹהֵינוּ **and Your praise, our God, Source of all powers and abilities,**

מִפִּינוּ לֹא יָמוּשׁ **will not depart from our lips**

לְעוֹלָם וָעֶד **forever and ever.**

We constantly praise Hashem for the past, the present, and the future.[8]

כִּי אֵל מֶלֶךְ

גָּדוֹל וְקָדוֹשׁ אָתָּה **For You are the Almighty, great and holy King.**

בָּרוּךְ אַתָּה **Blessed are You,**

יהוה **Master of the Universe, Who was, is, and always will be,**

(Between Rosh Hashanah and Yom Kippur)

הָאֵל הַקָּדוֹשׁ	הַמֶּלֶךְ הַקָּדוֹשׁ
The Almighty, the Holy One.	**The King, the Holy One.**
	We stand before You in judgment.

Amen: *It is true, and I believe with complete faith, that You are Holy and that it is impossible to perceive Your holiness.*[11]

Made a mistake? See page 134

אַתָּה קָדוֹשׁ **You are Holy**

Hashem is the source of all holiness and spiritual inspiration.

וְשִׁמְךָ קָדוֹשׁ **and Your Name[9] is Holy,**

A name is not a random title, but rather the definition and description of one's character and capabilities. A name contains the potential greatness inherent in a person. Therefore, the very Name of Hashem defines the ultimate holiness He is.

וּקְדוֹשִׁים בְּכָל יוֹם
יְהַלְלוּךָ סֶּלָה **and holy ones praise You every day, forever.**

Hashem has designated us His "holy ones."[10] His loving devotion to us is never-ending. How can we not praise Him every day, forever?

בָּרוּךְ אַתָּה **Blessed are You,**

יהוה **Master of the Universe, Who was, is, and always will be,**

(Between Rosh Hashanah and Yom Kippur)

הָאֵל הַקָּדוֹשׁ
The Almighty, the Holy One.

הַמֶּלֶךְ הַקָּדוֹשׁ
The King, the Holy One.
We stand before You in judgment.

> Made a mistake? See page 134

Amen: *It is true, and I believe with complete faith, that You are Holy and that it is impossible to perceive Your holiness.*[11]

൫ 4: Prayer for Insight ൡ

אַתָּה חוֹנֵן **You graciously grant**

לְאָדָם דַּעַת **knowledge to mankind**

Hashem grants us intelligence which surpasses that of all other living things. This is a special gift. All knowledge, from the ability to memorize our own name, to our understanding of the most complex mathematical equations, is a gift from Hashem. Our capacity to comprehend, calculate, decide, recognize, and remember is part of this gift. Even something as basic as our sense of direction — which enables us to know where we are, where to go, and how to get back — is also from Hashem.

וּמְלַמֵּד לָאֱנוֹשׁ בִּינָה **and teach insight to man.**

Without intelligence, a human being would be no greater than a living tree. The human mind is the greatest organ of intelligence in the physical world, and is capable of processing and storing mass amounts of information. We call this collection of information "knowledge." Hashem is the source of all knowledge and makes His knowledge available to everyone. If we extend ourselves to our utmost to use whatever knowledge we possess in service of Hashem and in adherence to Torah precepts to the point where it is only our own limits which prevent us from further growth, then Hashem will open our minds to more knowledge and a deeper insight to that which we already know, giving us a chance to increase our spiritual growth.[1]

The gift of comprehension plays an important part in our life. Comprehension leads to awareness and awareness is essential for spiritual success.[2] The greater your awareness of who you are, what you are, and why, the more you will be led to greater understanding of Hashem and the world He created.

The following is added during the Ma'ariv following a Shabbos or Yom Tov

אַתָּה חוֹנַנְתָּנוּ **You have graced us**

לְמַדַע תּוֹרָתֶךְ **[with the wisdom and insight] to know your Torah**

וַתְּלַמְּדֵנוּ לַעֲשׂוֹת **and you have taught us to fulfill**

חֻקֵּי רְצוֹנֶךְ **the statutes of Your will.**

Even if we do not understand Your statutes, we will perform them anyway, since it is Your will.[3]

Forgot to say this? See page 151

וַתַּבְדֵּל **You have distinguished,**

יהוה **Master of the Universe, Who was, is, and always will be,**

אֱלֹהֵינוּ **our God, Source of all powers and abilities,**

בֵּין קֹדֶשׁ לְחוֹל **between holy and unsanctified,**

"...to distinguish between the holy and the unsanctified..."[4]

בֵּין אוֹר לְחֹשֶׁךְ **between light and darkness,**

"and Hashem separated between the light and the darkness." [5]

בֵּין יִשְׂרָאֵל לָעַמִּים **between Yisrael and the nations,**

"You shall be holy for Me, for I, Hashem, am holy, and I separated you from the nations to be Mine." [6]

בֵּין יוֹם הַשְּׁבִיעִי **between the seventh day**

לְשֵׁשֶׁת יְמֵי הַמַּעֲשֶׂה **and the six days of work.**

"...for six days Hashem made the heaven and the earth, but on the seventh day, He ceased working and rested from the physical." [7]

Hashem designated the Sabbath to be unique by separating it from and exalting it above the other six days of the week. So, too, Hashem has made us special by distinguishing us from the other nations, choosing us to be the light of the darkness and the holiness of the unsanctified.

אָבִינוּ מַלְכֵּנוּ **Our Father, our King,**

הָחֵל עָלֵינוּ **begin for us**

הַיָּמִים הַבָּאִים לִקְרָאתֵנוּ **the days approaching us**

לְשָׁלוֹם **for peace,**

חֲשׂוּכִים מִכָּל חֵטְא **free of all sins,**

resistant to wrongdoing

וּמְנֻקִּים מִכָּל עָוֹן **cleansed of all iniquity,**

וּמְדֻבָּקִים בְּיִרְאָתֶךָ **and attached to the fear of You.**

D'veikus — attachment — is defined as being so devoted to a particular idea that you are unable to take any interest in anything else whatsoever.[8] We ask Hashem to assist us in the difficult task of fearing Him and His unlimited abilities. Only with Hashem's assistance will we be able to reach the ultimate goal of bonding ourselves to Fear of Heaven and Sin, to the extent where it is our essence.

וְחָנֵּנוּ מֵאִתְּךָ דֵּעָה **And graciously grant us from Yourself knowledge,**

בִּינָה וְהַשְׂכֵּל **insight, and wisdom.**

So that we may broaden our understanding and awareness of what is beneficial and what is harmful, what is right and what is wrong, improving and expanding our dedication to You and our adherence to the Torah You gave us.

בָּרוּךְ אַתָּה **Blessed are You,**

יהוה **Master of the Universe, Who was, is, and always will be,**

חוֹנֵן הַדָּעַת **gracious Granter of knowledge.**

CONTINUE WITH:

הֲשִׁיבֵנוּ אָבִינוּ **Return us, our Father,**

ON PAGE 54

חָנֵּנוּ מֵאִתְּךָ דֵּעָה **Graciously grant us from Yourself knowledge,**

בִּינָה וְהַשְׂכֵּל **insight, and wisdom.**

So that we may broaden our understanding and awareness of what is beneficial and what is harmful, what is right and what is wrong, improving and expanding our dedication to You and our adherence to the Torah You gave us.[9]

בָּרוּךְ אַתָּה **Blessed are You,**

יהוה **Master of the Universe, Who was, is, and always will be,**

חוֹנֵן הַדָּעַת **gracious Granter of knowledge.**

Amen: *It is true, and I believe with complete faith, that You graciously grant knowledge. May it be Your will[10] to grant us knowledge to serve You truthfully.*[11]

ca 5: Prayer for Repentance 80

Careful use of our intelligence would reveal how far we have strayed
from serving Hashem truthfully. We would see the negative effects this
irresponsibility has on ourselves, on the world, and on our special
relationship with Hashem.[1] Acknowledging that we have betrayed the
great pride Hashem has in us, we request:

הֲשִׁיבֵנוּ אָבִינוּ **Return us, our Father,**

לְתוֹרָתֶךְ **to Your Torah,**

Hashem created the world for one
purpose: that the Jewish people receive
the Torah and willingly obligate
themselves to its contents. Judaism is not
just a religion of humanity, but a *definition*
of humanity. Hashem foresaw the
problems that would plague our societies
and fashioned the Torah on the very
principles which can prevent them.
Realizing the root of our problems, we
ask our Father in heaven to help us return
to the Source — the Torah — so that we
can renew ourselves.[2]

וְקָרְבֵנוּ מַלְכֵּנוּ **and bring us near, our King,**

לַעֲבוֹדָתֶךְ **to Your service.**

To show our true desire to return to
Him, we ask Hashem, our King, to help
us serve Him by fulfilling His mitzvos in a
dedicated manner, as would a devoted
subject who wished to show his loyalty to
the king.[3]

וְהַחֲזִירֵנוּ **And bring us back**

בִּתְשׁוּבָה שְׁלֵמָה **in wholehearted repentance**

לְפָנֶיךָ **before You.**

We are stubborn. We take steps to repent, yet at the same time refuse to relinquish our bad habits completely. This causes us to stumble back into our old rut. We therefore ask Hashem to help us make our repentance complete and pure, so that we may forsake our past ways forever.[4]

We can all testify to how hard it is to change patterns of behavior. This is why we ask for Hashem's assistance. All He asks is that we take the first honest step in the right direction. Then He will assist us[5] not only in reaching our individual goals, but also in retaining them.

בָּרוּךְ אַתָּה **Blessed are You,**

יהוה **Master of the Universe, Who was, is, and always will be,**

הָרוֹצֶה בִּתְשׁוּבָה **Who desires repentance.**

You, Hashem, desire that we be close to You.[6]

Amen: *It is true, and I believe with complete faith, that You desire the repentance of wrongdoers. May it be Your will to accept us also with repentance.*[7]

ଓ 6: Prayer for Forgiveness ଞ

If we truly wish to return to Hashem, we must detach ourselves from the very entity that leads us astray.[1]

סְלַח לָנוּ אָבִינוּ **Forgive us, our Father,**

כִּי חָטָאנוּ **for we have unintentionally[2] sinned;**

We are in effect saying to Hashem, Father in heaven, have compassion on Your children and forgive us, for we have erred and caused You unhappiness.

מְחַל לָנוּ מַלְכֵּנוּ **pardon us, Our King,**

כִּי פָשָׁעְנוּ **for we have willfully[3] sinned,**

When we rebel against Hashem and intentionally transgress His will, we sever our parent-child relationship and reduce ourselves to the status of a king's servants who plead to have their sentence pardoned.[4]

כִּי מוֹחֵל וְסוֹלֵחַ אָתָּה **for You are Pardoner and Forgiver.**

Only Hashem's unparalleled depth of understanding can possibly acquit us of our constant wrongdoing and even eradicate it as though it never existed. Hashem makes this possible only if we fulfill three conditions: We must regret our past wrongdoing;[5] we must promise not to sin in the future nor to place ourselves in a situation where we might come to sin;[6] and we must actually change our bad ways to good.

בָּרוּךְ אַתָּה **Blessed are You,**

יהוה **Master of the Universe, Who was, is, and always will be,**

חַנּוּן הַמַּרְבֶּה לִסְלֹחַ **Gracious One, Who abundantly forgives.**

Forgiving is part of Your ongoing graciousness. It allows us to put aside our past and get a fresh start on the future.[7]

Amen: *It is true, and I believe with complete faith, that You abundantly forgive. May it be Your will to also forgive us for our unintentional and willful sins.*[8]

❧ 7: **Prayer for Salvation** ❧

It is sin that caused the exile we still endure. Our will to correct the cause of our long exile amongst the nations is the key to our redemption from it and our ongoing suffering.

רְאֵה [נָא] בְעָנְיֵנוּ **Look [please] upon our affliction**
Remove from us the day-to-day burdens and hardships that come our way.[1]

וְרִיבָה רִיבֵנוּ **and fight our battle,**
As Jews in exile, we suffer greatly at the hands of the nations oppressing us.[2]

וּגְאָלֵנוּ מְהֵרָה **and redeem us speedily**
Take notice of our merits and quickly bring us a redemption by reducing our suffering.[3]

לְמַעַן שְׁמֶךָ **for the sake of Your Name,**
(See "For the sake of His Name" page 37).[4]

כִּי גוֹאֵל חָזָק אָתָּה **for You are a mighty Redeemer.**
You can bring about redemption single-handedly. You do not need anyone's help, nor can anyone hinder You.

בָּרוּךְ אַתָּה **Blessed are You,**

יהוה **Master of the Universe, Who was, is, and always will be,**

גוֹאֵל יִשְׂרָאֵל **Redeemer of Yisrael.**
Only You, Hashem, can possibly redeem us from our present predicament.

Amen: *It is true, and I believe with complete faith, that You constantly redeem us. May it be Your will to speedily redeem us from our suffering.*[5]

ఆ 8: Prayer for Healing ఴ

Deterioration of our physical state of being is detrimental to our spiritual growth. A healthy body is conducive to a healthy mind, and a healthy mind is a key ingredient in successful spiritual growth.[1]

רְפָאֵנוּ Heal us,

Heal us from our physical deterioration, so that we may be healthy and strong to serve You and fulfill Your mitzvos to the best of our ability.

יהוה Master of the Universe, Who was, is, and always will be,

Healing is beyond the decision-making power of physicians.[2] If Hashem wants a person to be healed then he will be healed, no matter what the circumstances; and, if it is decreed that a person remain ill, then all the medical treatments in the world will be of no use.

וְנֵרָפֵא and we will be healed;

No doctor in the world can guarantee a complete recovery or that an illness will not recur. Hashem's healing, though, is complete and final.[3]

הוֹשִׁיעֵנוּ וְנִוָּשֵׁעָה save us and we will be saved.

Save us from our spiritual deterioration.

כִּי תְהִלָּתֵנוּ אָתָּה For You are our praise

When we recover from illness we feel rejuvenated and joyful.[4] Should we not use this joy to praise the One who brought it about?

וְהַעֲלֵה רְפוּאָה שְׁלֵמָה and bring a full recovery

לְכָל מַכּוֹתֵינוּ **for all of our wounds.**

> Therefore, Hashem, grant us a complete recovery from our physical and spiritual[5] defects and allow us new spiritual growth, bringing us ever closer to You.

Optional Prayer

רְפָא נָא **Heal please**

for male	*for female*
(patient's name)	*(patient's name)*

בֶּן **the son of:**   בַּת **the daughter of:**

(mother's name)	*(mother's name)*

רְפוּאָה שְׁלֵמָה **a full recovery**

בְּתוֹךְ שְׁאָר **amongst the other**

חוֹלֵי יִשְׂרָאֵל **patients of Yisrael.**

כִּי אֵל **For You are the Almighty**

> There is no illness You cannot heal.[6]

מֶלֶךְ **King,**

> sole Ruler over healing,

רוֹפֵא נֶאֱמָן וְרַחֲמָן אַתָּה **trustworthy and merciful Healer.**

> We trust doctors to give us the best possible remedies. Sometimes this requires them to be merciless, for if they were too merciful, they would fall short of their duty to try the utmost to heal. Hashem, though, is able to combine both qualities.[7]

בָּרוּךְ אַתָּה **Blessed are You,**

יהוה **Master of the Universe, Who was, is, and always will be,**

רוֹפֵא חוֹלֵי **Healer of the sick**

עַמּוֹ יִשְׂרָאֵל **of His nation Yisrael.**

Amen: *It is true, and I believe with complete faith, that any cure comes from You. May it be Your will to heal us spiritually and physically.*[8]

❧ 9: Prayer for a Year of Prosperity ❧

Ample nourishment is an important factor in maintaining our health.

בָּרֵךְ עָלֵינוּ **Bless on our behalf,**
Bless for our sake.

יהוה **Master of the world, Who was, is, and always will be,**

אֱלֹהֵינוּ **Our God, Source of all powers and abilities,**

אֶת הַשָּׁנָה הַזֹּאת **this year,**
May this year be a blessed and successful year.[1]

וְאֶת כָּל מִינֵי תְבוּאָתָהּ **and all its types of produce**
When food is scarce, demand for it escalates. This, in turn, drives the cost of living upwards, causing those less prosperous much hardship. In asking Hashem to bless the year's produce, we are asking Him to bless the whole world with a year of prosperity. Then everyone will have the means to obtain proper and sufficient nourishment without difficulty.[2]

לְטוֹבָה **for benefit.**
Plentiful food is for our benefit in more than one way. History has shown that economic instability is usually blamed on the Jews, often leading to anti-Semitism, pogroms, and the death of innocent Jews. This is why we ask Hashem to bless the year with plenty, for our sake.

**During the rainy season
(See page 144)**

וְתֵן טַל וּמָטָר לִבְרָכָה

**And give dew and rain for
blessing**

Neither too much or too little, too
strong or too light or in the wrong
season — give each location
according to its needs.[3]

**During the dry season
(See page 142)**

וְתֵן בְּרָכָה

And give a blessing

A blessing of prosperity.

Made
a
mistake?
See page
142 & 144

עַל פְּנֵי הָאֲדָמָה   **on the face of the earth.**

וְשַׂבְּעֵנוּ מִטּוּבָהּ   **Satisfy us with its bounty**
The bounty of Eretz Yisrael.

וְשַׂבְּעֵנוּ מִטּוּבֶךְ   **Satisfy us with Your bounty**
We must remember that the true
source of our bounty and prosperity is
Hashem, Who only uses the earth as a
means of relaying them to us.

וּבָרֵךְ שְׁנָתֵנוּ   **and bless our year**

כַּשָּׁנִים הַטּוֹבוֹת   **like the good years.**
Let each day be even more prosperous
than the previous one.[4]

בָּרוּךְ אַתָּה   **Blessed are You,**

יהוה   **Master of the Universe, Who was,
is, and always will be,**

מְבָרֵךְ הַשָּׁנִים   **Blesser of the years.**

Amen: *It is true, and I believe with complete faith, that You bless the
years. May it be Your will that this year be blessed.*[5]

ℭ 10: Ingather our People ℬ

During our long exile we have been prey to the brutality and hatred of the nations. With this in mind, we ask Hashem to redeem us from our painful exile, liberating us from foreign rule, thus fulfilling the prophecy of Yeshayah: "And it will come to pass on that day that a great shofar will be sounded and those who were lost in the land of Ashur and those who were dispersed in the land of Egypt shall come, and they will worship Hashem on the holy mountain in Yerushalayim."[1]

תְּקַע בְּשׁוֹפָר
גָּדוֹל לְחֵרוּתֵנוּ

Sound the great shofar to our freedom

Fulfill the prophecy of our prophets and free us from our exhausting bondage.

וְשָׂא נֵס
לְקַבֵּץ גָּלֻיּוֹתֵינוּ

and raise the banner

to gather our exiles.

Raise the banner to all the nations, signaling the beginning of our ingathering, as is stated in Yeshayah: "...and He shall raise a banner for the nations and will assemble the outcasts of Yisrael and gather together the dispersed of Yehudah from the four corners of the earth."[2]

וְקַבְּצֵנוּ יַחַד
מֵאַרְבַּע כַּנְפוֹת הָאָרֶץ

And gather us in unity

from the four corners of the earth.

We ask Hashem to "gather us in unity." Unity is the key to our nation's greatness. Unity enabled us to reach our highest level of glory, which we achieved when receiving the Torah on Mt. Sinai, where we stood united as one, with one heart[3] dedicated and ready to serve Hashem. Only when our love and sensitivity for another Jew faded, crippling our unity, did Hashem destroy the second *Beis Hamikdash* (which itself represented unity), thereby casting us into the exile of all exiles. Today, especially, when each Jewish community throughout the world has developed its own customs and traditions, we need to call upon Hashem to help us overcome our diversity and reunite us in harmony.

בָּרוּךְ אַתָּה **Blessed are You,**

יהוה **Master of the Universe, Who was, is, and always will be,**

מְקַבֵּץ נִדְחֵי **Gatherer of the dispersed**

עַמּוֹ יִשְׂרָאֵל **of His nation Yisrael.**

Hashem will gather all of His exiled people (even those who lack the knowledge that they are Jewish), including the ten tribes[4] who were dispersed to the point where their identity has become lost and unknown.

Amen: *It is true, and I believe with complete faith, that You will gather the dispersed of Your nation Yisrael. May it be Your will to speedily gather us.*[5]

ೞ 11: Restore True Justice ೫

Hashem's holy presence will never come to rest upon the Jewish nation until the corrupt judicial and law enforcement systems, which continue to add havoc to the prejudice that surrounds us, are eradicated and the Sanhedrin is reestablished.[1]

הָשִׁיבָה שׁוֹפְטֵינוּ
כְּבָרִאשׁוֹנָה

Restore our judges as at first

Only Hashem, Who is pure and incorruptible, can reinstate the true justice of the Sanhedrin that once was[2], as He has promised.[3]

וְיוֹעֲצֵינוּ כְּבַתְּחִלָּה

and our advisers as of yore,

The prophets of earlier times were the advisers[4] of our nation. Their advice and decisions were directed by Hashem and were thus unerring and universally accepted. Not so today, when each of the diverse groups making up modern-day Jewry has its own advisers to offer counsel, none of whom are universally accepted. This causes differences and unnecessary friction within the Jewish people.

וְהָסֵר מִמֶּנּוּ

and remove from us

יָגוֹן וַאֲנָחָה

sorrow and sighing.

In restoring our judges and advisers, You will remove the grief and agony we suffer, thereby laying the foundation for a sound and peaceful society.[5]

וּמְלוֹךְ עָלֵינוּ

And rule over us,

אַתָּה יהוה

You, Master of the Universe, Who was, is, and always will be,

לְבַדְּךָ **alone,**

Only after being painfully mistreated under the rule of other law systems will we appreciate the unique justice of the Almighty, our King.[6]

בְּחֶסֶד **with kindness**

Hashem understands our imperfection and is willing to judge us favorably even when we are unworthy.

וּבְרַחֲמִים **and with mercy,**

And even when we are to be punished, Hashem forgoes the deserved punishment and substitutes a more lenient one.[7]

וְצַדְּקֵנוּ בַּמִּשְׁפָּט **and find us righteous during judgment.**

Hashem will bring judgment upon the whole world, at which time each and every person will have to account for his actions. We ask Hashem not to look at our wrongdoing, but rather to regard all the suffering we have gone through, and find us righteous.

בָּרוּךְ אַתָּה **are You,**

יהוה **Master of the Universe, Who was, is, and always will be,**

מֶלֶךְ אוֹהֵב צְדָקָה וּמִשְׁפָּט
Lover of righteousness and justice.

Hashem's whole passion is to judge righteously. If only we would be the same!

(Between Rosh Hashanah and Yom Kippur)

הַמֶּלֶךְ הַמִּשְׁפָּט
The King of justice.

We stand before You in judgment.[8]

> Made a mistake? See page 135

Amen: *It is, true and I believe with complete faith, that You love righteousness and justice. May it be Your will to make us righteous in judgment.*[9]

✂ 12: Eradicate the Heretics ✂

Even an impeccable judicial system would not deter antagonists from continuously trying to eradicate our traditions or existence.

וְלַמַּלְשִׁינִים **And for informers**

אַל תְּהִי תִקְוָה **let there be no hope,**

Their constant slander, fabricated accusations, and informing on our religious activities has taken its toll in every generation. We ask Hashem to foil their evil intentions and cause them to stumble in their wickedness.

וְכָל הָרִשְׁעָה **and may all the wickedness**

כְּרֶגַע תֹּאבֵד **perish instantly,**

As a rule, we ask Hashem to do away with wickedness, not the wicked. The Talmud[1] relates that Rabbi Meir suffered so greatly from evil-hearted men who lived in his neighborhood that he prayed for them to die. His wife Beruria, though, understood from a verse in *Tehillim*[2] that we should not pray for the wicked to die, but rather for their sins to cease, so that they will no longer be wicked. After hearing this, Rabbi Meir began to pray for their repentance, and eventually, they did repent. We learn from this incident that we should pray only for end to the wickedness itself, not for the destruction of the evil-doer, who can repent.[3]

וְכָל אוֹיְבֶיךָ **and may all Your enemies**

מְהֵרָה יְכָּרֵתוּ **be speedily cut down.**

Since our enemies are Your enemies, bring down the physical threat of Your enemies, paralyzing their ability to harm us.[4]

וְהַזֵּדִים מְהֵרָה תְעַקֵּר **And may You speedily uproot,**
וּתְשַׁבֵּר וּתְמַגֵּר וְתַכְנִיעַ **smash, cast down, and humble the**
בִּמְהֵרָה בְיָמֵינוּ **insolent desecrators, speedily in**
our days.

Evil must be driven out to the point where not even a trace remains. Leaving behind even the smallest amount might enable its regeneration. (The same applies to uprooting a negative character trait. Suppressing it only helps for the short term. To really eradicate a negative trait a person must dedicate himself to totally removing it from his personality.)

בְּרוּךְ אַתָּה **Blessed are You,**

יהוה **Master of the Universe, Who was, is, and always will be,**

שׁוֹבֵר אוֹיְבִים **Smasher of enemies**

וּמַכְנִיעַ זֵדִים **and Humbler of the insolent desecrators.**

Amen: *It is true, and I believe with complete faith, that You smash the enemy. May it be Your will to speedily smash and humble them.*[5]

⚘ 13: Have Mercy on the Righteous ⚘

After the fall of the wicked, the truly righteous will rise and stand alone, acting as the "skyline" for our new and just society.[1]

עַל הַצַּדִּיקִים **Upon the righteous,**

וְעַל הַחֲסִידִים **and upon the devout,**

וְעַל זִקְנֵי **and upon the elders**
the Torah leaders of each generation[2]

עַמְּךָ בֵּית יִשְׂרָאֵל **of Your people, the House of Yisrael,**

וְעַל פְּלֵיטַת סוֹפְרֵיהֶם **and upon the remnant of their scholars,**
who teach the Torah and our tradition to the next generation.[3]

וְעַל גֵּרֵי הַצֶּדֶק **and upon the righteous converts,**
Hashem created the world based on His Master Plan of existence. Each and every one of us plays a unique, individual role in this Master Plan. Our goal in our lifetime is to carry out that very role, thus serving Hashem to our fullest ability. By doing so, we complete our piece of the Master Plan and fulfill our purpose in life. The individuals mentioned in this prayer work fervently to complete their goal; they restrain the evil inclination from enticing them with the trivialities that permeate society and keep us from completing our work.[4] These are the people for whom the world exists.

וְעָלֵינוּ **and upon us**
At the bottom of this social categorization are the average Jews who

lose their bearings on occasion, thereby allowing the evil inclination to distract them from their true purpose in life. Misled from the truth, they labor in the wrong direction and fall short of completing their goal. We must ask ourselves, "Where do I stand? What are my priorities in life?"

יֶהֱמוּ [נָא] רַחֲמֶיךָ **arouse [please] Your mercy,**

Have mercy on these important individuals who labor endlessly to ensure the ongoing fulfillment of the Master Plan and the Torah on which it is based. Hashem, You appreciate these great people more than we do; we are not deserving of them. At the same time, we ask You to have mercy on us as well and not to take them from our midst, for it is only through their merit that we exist.[5]

יהוה **Master of the Universe, Who was, is, and always will be,**

אֱלֹהֵינוּ **Our God, Source of all powers and abilities.**

וְתֵן שָׂכָר טוֹב **And give good reward**

לְכָל הַבּוֹטְחִים
בְּשִׁמְךָ בֶּאֱמֶת **to all those who sincerely trust in Your Name,**

Reward these great individuals for their ongoing efforts by easing their hardship which drains them from being able to serve the needs of the nation.

וְשִׂים חֶלְקֵינוּ **and place our lot**

עִמָּהֶם לְעוֹלָם **with them forever**

Shower us with Your overwhelming Divine Providence and help us also to sincerely trust in Your Name,[6] to firmly believe that You are the Source of all powers and abilities, and Master of the Universe, Who was, is, and always will be, so that our lot will also be amongst those who merit greatness in the World to Come.

וְלֹא נֵבוֹשׁ **and we will not feel ashamed,**

כִּי בְךָ בָטָחְנוּ **for in You we trust.**

There are occasions when we are ashamed of being Jewish and even stoop so low as to hide our identity. But trusting in You will give us the understanding of who we are, so that we will appreciate and be proud of our heritage and never be ashamed of it.[7]

בָּרוּךְ אַתָּה **Blessed are You,**

יהוה **Master of the Universe, Who was, is, and always will be,**

מִשְׁעָן וּמִבְטָח **the Support and Trust**

לַצַּדִּיקִים **of the righteous.**

Amen: It is true, and I believe with complete faith, that You are the Support and Trust of the righteous. May it be Your will to support us also.[8]

ಝ 14: Rebuild the Holy Yerushalayim ಝ

At the center of this new and just society will stand the re-glorified city Yerushalayim.

When the Beis Hamikdash stood, Yerushalayim was known as the most glorious city both in spiritual exaltedness and in physical beauty. People used to flock from all over the world to gaze at the city's elegance and feel it's radiance. Hashem was dwelling in His palace — His chosen city.

וְלִירוּשָׁלַיִם עִירְךָ **And to Yerushalayim, Your city,**

בְּרַחֲמִים תָּשׁוּב **return with mercy,**

Upon the destruction of the *Beis Hamikdash*, Hashem left His dwelling place amongst His chosen nation, leaving Yerushalayim in desolation. The prophet Yirmiyahu, in the book of *Eichah*, describes Yerushalayim's anguish as she lies in her desolation, defiled and weeping bitterly, waiting to have her glory restored. We ask Hashem to have mercy on the city and return it to its former glory.[1]

וְתִשְׁכֹּן בְּתוֹכָהּ **and dwell within it**

כַּאֲשֶׁר דִּבַּרְתָּ **as You have spoken,**

And dwell within it once again, just as You said to the prophet Zechariah, "I have returned to Zion, and I will dwell within Yerushalayim, and Yerushalayim shall be called The City of Truth."[2]

וּבְנֵה אוֹתָהּ **and build it**

בְּקָרוֹב בְּיָמֵינוּ **soon in our days**

The rebuilding of Yerushalayim, with the erecting of the third *Beis Hamikdash*, will climax our people's return to their land at the end of our exile.

בִּנְיַן עוֹלָם **as an everlasting structure,**

The first and second *Beis Hamikdash*, having been built by man, were susceptible to destruction by man. The third *Beis Hamikdash*, though, will be erected by Hashem, and will thus be everlasting and indestructible.[3]

וְכִסֵּא דָוִד **and the throne of David**

מְהֵרָה לְתוֹכָהּ תָּכִין **speedily establish within it.**

The restoration of Yerushalayim could not be complete without the re-establishment of the Davidic dynasty — with the ascent of *Mashiach*, descendant of King David. The sooner Hashem brings about these preparations, the sooner will be the end to our exile.

נַחֵם Mourning the Destruction of Yerushalayim
Added here on Tish'ah b'Av, during Minchah

נַחֵם **Console**

יהוה **Master of the Universe, Who was, is, and always will be,**

אֱלֹהֵינוּ **our God, Source of all powers and abilities,**

אֶת אֲבֵלֵי צִיּוֹן **the mourners of Zion**

The mourners of the spiritual ruin of Zion.[4]

וְאֶת אֲבֵלֵי יְרוּשָׁלָיִם **and the mourners of Yerushalayim**

וְאֶת הָעִיר **and the city**

Forgot to say this? See page 146

הָאֲבֵלָה וְהַחֲרֵבָה   **that is in mourning and ruins,**

וְהַבְּזוּיָה וְהַשּׁוֹמֵמָה   **degraded and desolate,**

הָאֲבֵלָה מִבְּלִי בָנֶיהָ   **mourning without her children,**
        Yisrael,

וְהַחֲרֵבָה מִמְּעוֹנוֹתֶיהָ   **devastated of her dwellings,**
        that were detroyed,[5]

וְהַבְּזוּיָה מִכְּבוֹדָהּ   **degraded from her glory**
        as it states, "All who once respected
her, degrade her, for they have seen her
disgrace." [6]

וְהַשּׁוֹמֵמָה מֵאֵין יוֹשֵׁב   **and desolate of inhabitants.**
        as it states, "How does it come to be
that she sits in solitude? The city that was
great with people has become like a
widow."[7]

וְהִיא יוֹשֶׁבֶת   **And she sits**

וְרֹאשָׁהּ חָפוּי   **with her head covered**

כְּאִשָּׁה עֲקָרָה   **like a barren woman**

שֶׁלֹּא יָלְדָה   **who has never given birth.**
        Her pain is like that of a married woman
who is barren. With her head drooping to
the ground, she sits anguished over her
misfortune.

וַיְבַלְּעוּהָ לִגְיוֹנוֹת   **Legions have devoured her**

וַיִּירָשׁוּהָ עוֹבְדֵי זָרִים   **and idolaters have taken her over.**

וַיַּטִּילוּ אֶת   **They have taken**

עַמְּךָ יִשְׂרָאֵל   **Your Nation Yisrael**

לֶחָרֶב   **to the sword**

וַיַּהַרְגוּ בְזָדוֹן   **and have intentionally murdered**

חֲסִידֵי עֶלְיוֹן the devoted of the Supreme One.

עַל כֵּן Therefore,

צִיּוֹן בְּמַר תִּבְכֶּה Zion weeps bitterly
> as it states, "She weeps bitterly in the night and her tear is on her cheek."[8]

וִירוּשָׁלַיִם תִּתֵּן קוֹלָהּ and Yerushalayim raises her voice,
> and wails in great pain like a woman giving birth for the first time,[9]

לִבִּי לִבִּי עַל חַלְלֵיהֶם "My heart, My heart [writhes] for the slain,
> for the brutally murdered,[10]

מֵעַי מֵעַי עַל חַלְלֵיהֶם my innards, my innards [ache] for the slain."
> for the corpses that litter the environs of Yerushalayim.[11]

כִּי אַתָּה For You,

יהוה Master of the Universe, Who was, is, and always will be,

בָּאֵשׁ הִצַּתָּהּ consumed her with fire
> as it states, "Hashem extinguished His fury, He poured out His fierce anger, He kindled a fire in Zion which consumed its foundations."[12]

וּבָאֵשׁ אַתָּה and with fire You will

עָתִיד לִבְנוֹתָהּ in the future rebuild her

כָּאָמוּר as it is said,

וַאֲנִי אֶהְיֶה לָּהּ "I will be to her,

נְאֻם יהוה says the Master of the Universe, Who was, is, and always will be,

חוֹמַת אֵשׁ סָבִיב **a wall of fire around,**

וּלְכָבוֹד אֶהְיֶה בְּתוֹכָהּ **and I will be glorious in her midst."**[13]

בָּרוּךְ אַתָּה **Blessed are You,**

יהוה **Master of the Universe, Who was, is, and always will be,**

מְנַחֵם צִיּוֹן **Consoler of Zion**

וּבוֹנֵה יְרוּשָׁלָיִם **and Builder of Yerushalayim.**

as it states, "For Hashem will console Zion, He will console all its ruins, and he will make its deserts like Eden and its arid land like the Garden of Hashem; joy and happiness shall be found therein, thanksgiving and a voice of melody."[14]

Amen: *It is true, and I believe with complete faith, that You will console Zion and rebuild Yerushalayim. May it be Your will to console Zion and rebuild Yerushalayim speedily in our days.*

CONTINUE WITH:

אֶת צֶמַח דָּוִד **The sprout of David,**

ON PAGE 79

בָּרוּךְ אַתָּה **Blessed are You,**

יהוה **Master of the Universe, Who was, is, and always will be,**

בּוֹנֵה יְרוּשָׁלָיִם **Builder of Yerushalayim.**

Amen: *It is true, and I believe with complete faith, that You will rebuild Yerushalayim. May it be Your will to speedily rebuild it for the sake of Your Name.*[15]

⊰ 15: The Davidic Dynasty ⊱

Mashiach will arrive and reign as king of the Jewish people in the land of the nation of *Yisrael*, thereby completing the Redemption.

אֶת צֶמַח דָּוִד **The sprout of David,**

עַבְדְּךָ **Your servant,**

מְהֵרָה תַצְמִיחַ **speedily cause to sprout**

We mentioned earlier (see "and causes salvation to sprout forth" page 43) that the Final Redemption with the coming of *Mashiach* will be brought about gradually. We ask Hashem to speed up the sprouting process, to bring *Mashiach* quickly.

וְקַרְנוֹ תָּרוּם בִּישׁוּעָתֶךָ **and exalt his power with Your deliverance,**

Deliver us from our exile of oppression and degradation with the exalting of *Mashiach*, who with his God-given powers will show the entire world our legitimacy as the chosen nation.

כִּי לִישׁוּעָתְךָ

קִוִּינוּ כָּל הַיּוֹם **for we await Your salvation all day long.**

At the end of our life (may we live to 120 years) when our day of judgment arrives, the heavenly court will ask each one of us, "Did you yearn for the Final Redemption?"[1] Those who yearn and wait for the Redemption will be showered by Hashem with an abundance of goodness in the World to Come, while those who did not, or those who had doubts, will lose their share to the righteous.[2] We must ask ourselves: Do I truly yearn and wait for the Final Redemption?

בָּרוּךְ אַתָּה **Blessed are You,**

יהוה **Master of the Universe, Who was, is, and always will be,**

מַצְמִיחַ קֶרֶן

יְשׁוּעָה **Causer of the power of salvation to sprout forth.**

Amen: *It is true, and I believe with complete faith, that You will cause our salvation to sprout forth. May it be Your will to do this speedily in our days.*[3]

ೞ 16: Accept our Prayers ೞ

Our needs have been expressed and we conclude with a plea that they be accepted.

שְׁמַע קוֹלֵנוּ **Hear our voice,**

יהוה **Master of the Universe, Who was, is, and always will be,**

אֱלֹהֵינוּ **Our God, Source of all powers and abilities.**

חוּס וְרַחֵם עָלֵינוּ **Pity us and be merciful to us,**

We ask Hashem to have pity and mercy on us, just as a father has for his children.[1]

וְקַבֵּל בְּרַחֲמִים **and accept, with mercy**

וּבְרָצוֹן **and with favor,**

אֶת תְּפִלָּתֵנוּ **our prayer.**

Even if we lack the merit, accept our prayer favorably.[2]

כִּי אֵל שׁוֹמֵעַ תְּפִלּוֹת
וְתַחֲנוּנִים אָתָּה **For You are the Almighty, Who hears prayers and appeals,**

וּמִלְּפָנֶיךָ מַלְכֵּנוּ **and from before You, our King,**

Even though we are not worthy of standing before You, King of all kings.

רֵיקָם אַל תְּשִׁיבֵנוּ **do not turn us away empty-handed.**

Now that we do stand before You, do not turn us away empty-handed, for we are helpless without You.[3]

The following is added here on fast days

עֲנֵנוּ   Answer us,

יהוה   Master of the Universe, Who was, is, and always will be,

עֲנֵנוּ   answer us

בְּיוֹם צוֹם תַּעֲנִיתֵנוּ   on the day of public gathering for our fasting[4]

כִּי בְצָרָה גְדוֹלָה אֲנָחְנוּ   for we are in great trouble.
Spiritually and physically.

אַל תֵּפֶן אֶל רִשְׁעֵנוּ   Do not regard our wickedness,
Overlook our wrongdoings.

וְאַל תַּסְתֵּר פָּנֶיךָ מִמֶּנּוּ   do not conceal Your Face from us
from our prayers,[5]

וְאַל תִּתְעַלַּם   and do not hide

מִתְּחִנָּתֵנוּ   from our supplication.

הֱיֵה נָא קָרוֹב   Please be near

לְשַׁוְעָתֵנוּ   to our outcry;

יְהִי נָא חַסְדְּךָ לְנַחֲמֵנוּ   please let Your lovingkindness console us.
Unveil your infinite compassion and wipe away our troubles and distress

טֶרֶם נִקְרָא אֵלֶיךָ   Even before we call to You,

עֲנֵנוּ   answer us,

כַּדָּבָר שֶׁנֶּאֱמַר   as it is said:

Forgot to say this? See page 147

וְהָיָה טֶרֶם יִקְרָאוּ **"And it will come to pass that when they have not yet called,** in supplication[6]

וַאֲנִי אֶעֱנֶה **I will answer;**

עוֹד הֵם מְדַבְּרִים **while they are yet speaking,** their prayer[7]

וַאֲנִי אֶשְׁמָע **I will hear."**[8]
Hashem desires to hear our prayers and constantly awaits their ascent.

כִּי אַתָּה **For You are**

יהוה **Master of the Universe, Who was, is, and always will be,**

הָעוֹנֶה בְּעֵת צָרָה **Who responds in time of trouble;**

פּוֹדֶה וּמַצִּיל **Who redeems and rescues**

בְּכָל עֵת צָרָה וְצוּקָה **in all times of trouble and distress.**

כִּי אַתָּה שׁוֹמֵעַ תְּפִלַּת **For You hear the prayer**

עַמְּךָ יִשְׂרָאֵל **of Your people, Yisrael,**

בְּרַחֲמִים **with mercy.**

בָּרוּךְ אַתָּה **Blessed are You,**

יהוה **Master of the Universe, Who was, is, and always will be,**

שׁוֹמֵעַ תְּפִלָּה **Hearer of prayer.**
"Prayer" in the singular, and not "prayers". Since we request not only for ourselves but also for the general public, our individual prayers are as one prayer.

Amen: *It is true, and I believe with complete faith, that You hear prayer. May it be Your will to hear our prayers.*[9]

❧ 17: Restore the Service of the ❧ Beis Hamikdash

The daily prayer service we have today was established as a temporary substitute for the daily sacrificial services in the *Beis Hamikdash*. With this in mind, we ask Hashem to reinstate the daily service of the *Beis Hamikdash*.[1]

רְצֵה **Be pleased**

יהוה **Master of the Universe, Who was, is, and always will be,**

אֱלֹהֵינוּ **our God, Source of all powers and abilities,**

בְּעַמְּךָ יִשְׂרָאֵל **with Your people, Yisrael,**

וּבִתְפִלָּתָם **and their prayer,**
the speedy return of the *Beis Hamikdash*.

וְהָשֵׁב **and restore**

אֶת הָעֲבוֹדָה **the priestly service**

לִדְבִיר בֵּיתֶךָ **to the Holy of Holies,[2]**
Restore the service of the *Beis Hamikdash* that was officiated in the Holy of Holies.

וְאִשֵּׁי יִשְׂרָאֵל **and the fire-offerings of Yisrael;**
And restore the sacrificial service of the *Beis Hamikdash* that was officiated outside the Holy of Holies.[3]

וּתְפִלָּתָם בְּאַהֲבָה
תְקַבֵּל בְּרָצוֹן **and accept their prayer favorably with love.**
Because of the love You have for Your people, accept their prayer favorably.[4]

וּתְהִי לְרָצוֹן תָּמִיד **And may the service of Your people**
עֲבוֹדַת יִשְׂרָאֵל עַמֶּךְ **Yisrael be favorable forever.**
May it never have to cease again.5

The following is added on Rosh Chodesh and Chol HaMoed

אֱלֹהֵינוּ **Our God, Source of all powers and abilities,**

וֵאלֹהֵי אֲבוֹתֵינוּ **and the God of our Forefathers,**

יַעֲלֶה וְיָבֹא **may they ascend and come,**
May our prayers rise up to heaven and arrive unhindered at the palace of the King.6

וְיַגִּיעַ וְיֵרָאֶה **arrive and appear,**
May nothing prevent them from reaching and entering the courtyard of the King, and receiving an audience with Him.6

וְיֵרָצֶה וְיִשָּׁמַע **be favorable and heard,**
May they appear before the King at a favorable time, so as to be heard and accepted.6

וְיִפָּקֵד וְיִזָּכֵר **be considered and be remembered,**
Consider our prayers and remember us.

זִכְרוֹנֵנוּ וּפִקְדוֹנֵנוּ **the remembrance and consideration of ourselves,**

וְזִכְרוֹן אֲבוֹתֵינוּ **the remembrance of our Forefathers**
Remember Your covenant with the Forefathers, as it states, "Remember Your servants Avraham, Yitzchak, and

Forgot to say this? See page 148

Yaakov. You swore to them by Your very essence and said to them: I will make your descendants as numerous as the stars of the sky, and all this land which I stated I will give to your offspring for them to inherit forever."[7]

וְזִכְרוֹן **and the remembrance of**

מָשִׁיחַ *Mashiach*

בֶּן דָּוִד עַבְדֶּךָ **the son of David, Your servant,**

וְזִכְרוֹן **the remembrance of**

יְרוּשָׁלַיִם *Yerushalayim*
that is in mourning and ruin,[8]

עִיר קָדְשֶׁךָ **the city of Your holiness,**
where Your Divine Presence once dwelled in the *Beis Hamikdash*.

וְזִכְרוֹן כָּל עַמְּךָ **and the remembrance of Your entire nation**
Remember Your covenant with the Jewish people, as it states, "For Hashem will not forsake His nation, and He will not abandon His inheritance."[9]

בֵּית יִשְׂרָאֵל לְפָנֶיךָ **the House of Yisrael, before You**

לִפְלֵיטָה לְטוֹבָה **for survival, for goodness,**

לְחֵן וּלְחֶסֶד **for graciousness, lovingkindness,**

וּלְרַחֲמִים **and mercy,**
Your entire spectrum of goodness,

לְחַיִּים **for life,**
life beginning in this world and continuing into the next — the World to Come,

וּלְשָׁלוֹם **and for peace,**
peaceful life and peace of mind,

(on Rosh Chodesh)

בְּיוֹם רֹאשׁ הַחֹדֶשׁ הַזֶּה **on this day, the beginning of the new month.**

(on Pesach)

בְּיוֹם חַג הַמַּצּוֹת הַזֶּה **on this day of the Festival of Matzahs.**

(on Succos)

בְּיוֹם חַג הַסֻּכּוֹת הַזֶּה **on this day of the Festival of Succos.**

זָכְרֵנוּ **Remember us,**

יהוה **Master of the Universe Who was, is, and always will be,**

אֱלֹהֵינוּ **our God, Source of all powers and abilities,**

בּוֹ לְטוֹבָה **on this day for good,**

The Torah is called good, as it states, "For I have given you a good acquisition, do not forsake my Torah."[10] Also, "It is a tree of life for those who cling to it, and its supporters are fortunate";[11] "Its ways are ways of pleasantness and all its paths are peace."[12] Because Torah is the true source of life, our need for it is continual. We therefore ask Hashem to remember our dependency on the Torah and to give us insight into its life-giving essence.

וּפָקְדֵנוּ בוֹ לִבְרָכָה **and consider us on this day for blessing,**

Prosperity allows us to serve Hashem in good health with peace of mind. We therefore take this opportunity to ask Hashem to consider us periodically and grant us blessing in our lives so that we will be able to dedicate ourselves to listening, learning, teaching, preserving, practicing, and fulfilling all the words of the Torah, with love and a sense of reverence.[13]

וְהוֹשִׁיעֵנוּ בוֹ לְחַיִּים **and deliver us on this day for life.**

as it states, "Hashem saves, the King will answer on the day we call."[14]

וּבִדְבַר יְשׁוּעָה **And concerning the matter of salvation**

וְרַחֲמִים **and mercy,**

חוּס וְחָנֵּנוּ **pity us and be gracious to us,**

as it states, "...and it will be when he cries out to Me, I will listen, for I am gracious."[15]

וְרַחֵם עָלֵינוּ **have mercy upon us**

take notice of our unfortunate state

וְהוֹשִׁיעֵנוּ **and save us.**

כִּי אֵלֶיךָ עֵינֵינוּ **For our eyes are turned towards You,**

As its states, I raise my eyes to the mountains; from where will come my help? My help is from Hashem, Maker of heaven and earth."[16]

כִּי אֵל מֶלֶךְ
חַנּוּן וְרַחוּם אָתָּה **for You are the Almighty, gracious and merciful King.**

Throughout history, only a precious few were given the privilege of seeing Hashem's Divine Presence. However, when Hashem returns to Zion (Yerushalayim) His presence will be visible to all, as it says in Yeshayah, "For they shall see eye to eye when Hashem returns to Zion."[17]

וְתֶחֱזֶינָה עֵינֵינוּ **And may our eyes see**

בְּשׁוּבְךָ לְצִיּוֹן **Your return to Zion**

May we merit not only to be present when You return to Yerushalayim, but to actually see Your Divine Presence.[18]

Seeing Hashem's Divine Presence is a special spiritual experience. Hashem warns us against gazing for pleasure at things that could jeopardize the Divine element within us. Those who do so, will not be allowed to take pleasure in seeing the Divine Presence — the apex of the spiritual.

בְּרַחֲמִים **with mercy.**

Those who are present when Hashem returns to Yerushalayim, yet who lack the means to see His Presence, will suffer endless agony. Have mercy on these people who are unaware of their shortcomings, and allow them also to see Your Divine Presence.

בָּרוּךְ אַתָּה **Blessed are You,**

יהוה **Master of the Universe, Who was, is, and always will be,**

הַמַּחֲזִיר שְׁכִינָתוֹ לְצִיּוֹן **Who returns His Divine Presence to Zion.**

Amen: *It is true, and I believe with complete faith, that You will return Your Divine Presence to Zion,*[19] *where it will be revealed to all.*[20]

basic 18: Prayer of Thankfulness basic

Of all the gifts Hashem grants us, there is none greater than the gift of life.

מוֹדִים אֲנַחְנוּ לָךְ **We are thankful to You**

שָׁאַתָּה הוּא **that You are the One Who is the**

יהוה **Master of the Universe, Who was, is, and always will be,**

אֱלֹהֵינוּ **our God, Source of all powers and abilities,**

וֵאלֹהֵי אֲבוֹתֵינוּ **and the God of our Forefathers,**

לְעוֹלָם וָעֶד **for ever and ever.**

How happy are we that You are God, Who runs the world and sees to everything.[1] Fortunate are we that You have chosen us to be Your people — we are proud of that honor.[2]

צוּר חַיֵּינוּ **Rock of our lives,**

"Rock" connotes stability and security, insurance against misfortune. No insurance agency on earth can really protect people from tragedy; it can only reimburse them financially for any loss suffered. Only Hashem can guarantee life (if He so wishes).[3]

מָגֵן יִשְׁעֵנוּ **Shield of our salvation,**

We live in a dangerous world where being in the wrong place at the wrong time can get us into trouble. What "insurance company" will be there to protect us and bring about our salvation? Only Hashem.[4]

אַתָּה הוּא **are You**

לְדוֹר וָדוֹר **from generation to generation.**

Only Hashem has arranged and guaranteed our continued existence throughout history.[5] We express our thanks to Him for being the "Rock of our lives" and the "Shield of our salvation."

נוֹדֶה לְּךָ **We give thanks to You**

וּנְסַפֵּר תְּהִלָּתֶךָ **and enumerate Your praise**

עַל חַיֵּינוּ **for our lives**

הַמְּסוּרִים בְּיָדֶךָ **that are given into Your hand,**

We offer thanks to Hashem for our physical existence, for He is the sole producer of life. Nothing lives unless Hashem wants it to.[6]

וְעַל נִשְׁמוֹתֵינוּ **and for our souls**

הַפְּקוּדוֹת לָךְ **that are entrusted to You,**

Each night while we sleep our soul returns to heaven to be entrusted to Hashem. Upon retiring we declare: "Into His hand I entrust my spirit when I go to sleep."[7] We offer You praise[8] for returning our soul to us each morning refreshed and ready to serve You another day.[9]

וְעַל נִסֶּיךָ **and for Your miracles**

שֶׁבְּכָל יוֹם עִמָּנוּ **that are with us every day,**

We thank You and enumerate Your praise for the miracles You perform through our own actions.[10]

וְעַל נִפְלְאוֹתֶיךָ **and for Your wonders**

And for the unnoticed wonders. We forget that nature itself is one vast miracle.

וְטוֹבוֹתֶיךָ **and Your favors**

For unearned favors as well, we offer our heartfelt thanks.[11]

שֶׁבְּכָל עֵת **which occur at every moment,**

עֶרֶב וָבֹקֶר **evening, morning**

וְצָהֳרָיִם **and noon.**

Which You perform for us at all times, each and every day.[12]

הַטּוֹב **The Virtuous One,**

כִּי לֹא כָלוּ רַחֲמֶיךָ **for Your mercy never ends**

Everything Hashem does is for our good. Many times we may be deserving of severe punishment or even, God forbid, death. Yet Hashem's never-ending compassion nullifies[13] these decrees and replaces them with everyday hardships such as minor injury, illness, or loss of money. Even though we look at these things negatively, they are really examples of Hashem's vast goodness and infinite compassion.

וְהַמְרַחֵם **and the Merciful One,**

כִּי לֹא תַמּוּ חֲסָדֶיךָ **for Your acts of kindness never cease.**

Your mercy is demonstrated by your constant acts of kindness towards us.

מֵעוֹלָם קִוִּינוּ לָךְ **We have always put our hope in You.**

We have always relied upon You to guide us through life.[14]

מודים דרבנן

מוֹדִים אֲנַחְנוּ לָךְ **We are thankful to You**

שָׁאַתָּה הוּא **that it is You Who is the**

יהוה **Master of the Universe, Who was, is, and always will be**

אֱלֹהֵינוּ **Our God, Source of all powers and abilities,**

וֵאלֹהֵי אֲבוֹתֵינוּ **and the God of our Forefathers,**

אֱלֹהֵי כָל בָּשָׂר **the God of all flesh,**

יוֹצְרֵנוּ **our Creator,**

יוֹצֵר בְּרֵאשִׁית **Maker of creation.**

בְּרָכוֹת וְהוֹדָאוֹת **Blessings and thanksgiving**

לְשִׁמְךָ הַגָּדוֹל וְהַקָּדוֹשׁ **to Your great and holy Name**

עַל שֶׁהֶחֱיִיתָנוּ **for keeping us alive**

וְקִיַּמְתָּנוּ **and sustaining us;**

כֵּן תְּחַיֵּנוּ וּתְקַיְּמֵנוּ **so may You always keep and sustain us.**

וְתֶאֱסוֹף גָּלֻיּוֹתֵינוּ **And gather our exiles**

לְחַצְרוֹת קָדְשֶׁךָ **to the courtyards of Your *Beis Hamikdash***

לִשְׁמוֹר חֻקֶּיךָ **to observe Your statutes,**

וְלַעֲשׂוֹת רְצוֹנֶךָ **to do Your will,**

וּלְעָבְדְּךָ בְּלֵבָב שָׁלֵם **and to serve You wholeheartedly,**

עַל שֶׁאֲנַחְנוּ מוֹדִים לָךְ **for that which we are grateful to You.**

    We are grateful to You for creating us and honoring us with the Torah of Truth, thereby setting us apart from those who go astray. May it be Your will to open our hearts to the truth of Your Torah so that we may appreciate the honor and serve You wholeheartedly.

בָּרוּךְ אֵל הַהוֹדָאוֹת **Blessed is the Almighty to Whom all thanks is due.**

The following is added on Chanukah and Purim

[וְ]עַל הַנִּסִּים **[And] for the miracles**

    [And] we thank You for the unmistakable act of intervention, Your Divine Providence.[15]

וְעַל הַפֻּרְקָן **and for the redemption**
from our enemy

וְעַל הַגְּבוּרוֹת **and for the mighty deeds**

וְעַל הַתְּשׁוּעוֹת **and for the deliverance**

וְעַל הַמִּלְחָמוֹת **and for the battles**

שֶׁעָשִׂיתָ לַאֲבוֹתֵינוּ **that You performed for our ancestors**

בַּיָּמִים הָהֵם בַּזְּמַן הַזֶּה **in those days at this time.**

Forgot to say this? See page 150

(On Chanukah)

בִּימֵי מַתִּתְיָהוּ In the days of Mattisyahu

בֶּן יוֹחָנָן the son of Yochanan

כֹּהֵן גָּדוֹל the High Priest,

חַשְׁמוֹנַאי וּבָנָיו the Chashmonean, and his sons,

כְּשֶׁעָמְדָה מַלְכוּת יָוָן

הָרְשָׁעָה when the evil Greek kingdom rose up

under the leadership of Antiochus IV

עַל עַמְּךָ יִשְׂרָאֵל against Your nation Yisrael

לְהַשְׁכִּיחָם תּוֹרָתֶךָ to make them forget Your Torah

וּלְהַעֲבִירָם and to turn them away

מֵחֻקֵּי רְצוֹנֶךָ from the statutes of Your will.

Forgot
to say
this?
See page
150

Antiochus decreed a total ban on Torah study so that the Jewish nation would forget the laws and succumb to the heavy influence of Greek culture — a culture that breathed and radiated immorality and profanity.[16]

וְאַתָּה And You,

בְּרַחֲמֶיךָ הָרַבִּים in Your abundant mercy

עָמַדְתָּ לָהֶם stood by them

בְּעֵת צָרָתָם in their time of suffering.

רַבְתָּ אֶת רִיבָם You defended their cause,

You brought an end to the evil decrees of the Greeks.[17]

דַּנְתָּ אֶת דִּינָם You judged their claim,

נָקַמְתָּ אֶת נִקְמָתָם and You avenged their wrong.

מָסַרְתָּ גִבּוֹרִים **You delivered the strong**

בְּיַד חַלָּשִׁים **into the hands of the weak,**

וְרַבִּים בְּיַד מְעַטִּים **the many into the hands of the few,**

וּטְמֵאִים **the impure**

בְּיַד טְהוֹרִים **into the hands of the pure,**

וּרְשָׁעִים **the wicked**

בְּיַד צַדִּיקִים **into the hands of the righteous,**

וְזֵדִים בְּיַד **and the insolent desecrators into the hands**

עוֹסְקֵי תוֹרָתֶךְ **of those who occupy themselves with Your Torah.**

וּלְךָ עָשִׂיתָ **For Yourself, You made**

שֵׁם גָּדוֹל וְקָדוֹשׁ **a great and sanctified Name**

בְּעוֹלָמֶךְ **in Your world,**
For then it was very clear that You, and only You, are the Ruler of the World.[18]

וּלְעַמְּךָ יִשְׂרָאֵל **and for Your nation Yisrael**

עָשִׂיתָ **You performed**

תְּשׁוּעָה גְדוֹלָה **a great deliverance**

וּפֻרְקָן כְּהַיּוֹם הַזֶּה **and salvation, as this day.**

וְאַחַר כֵּן בָּאוּ בָנֶיךָ **Afterwards, Your children came**

לִדְבִיר **to the Holy of Holies**

בֵּיתֶךָ **of Your House**

וּפִנּוּ אֶת הֵיכָלֶךָ **cleaned out Your Sanctuary,**
from the pagan idol worship of the Greeks

וְטִהֲרוּ אֶת מִקְדָּשֶׁךְ **purified Your *Beis Hamikdash*,**

וְהִדְלִיקוּ נֵרוֹת **and kindled lights**

בְּחַצְרוֹת קָדְשֶׁךְ **in the Courtyards of Your *Beis Hamikdash*,**

Through the hands of the Chashmoneans, Hashem rekindled the influence of Torah in the world, redeeming us from the bleak darkness of the immorality and profanity that pervaded our society.

וְקָבְעוּ **and established**

שְׁמוֹנַת יְמֵי

חֲנֻכָּה אֵלּוּ **these eight days of Chanukah**

לְהוֹדוֹת וּלְהַלֵּל **to express gratitude and praise**

לְשִׁמְךָ הַגָּדוֹל **to Your great Name.**

From the depth of our hearts we thank You for preserving our Torah heritage.

Forgot to say this? See page 150

(On Purim)

בִּימֵי מָרְדְּכַי **In the days of Mordechai**

וְאֶסְתֵּר **and Esther**

בְּשׁוּשַׁן הַבִּירָה **in Shushan the capital**

כְּשֶׁעָמַד עֲלֵיהֶם

הָמָן הָרָשָׁע **when Haman the wicked rose up against them,**

בִּקֵּשׁ לְהַשְׁמִיד **he sought to destroy,**

לַהֲרוֹג וּלְאַבֵּד **kill, and annihilate**

אֶת כָּל הַיְּהוּדִים **all the Jews**

מִנַּעַר וְעַד זָקֵן **from young to old,**

טַף וְנָשִׁים **infants and women,**

בְּיוֹם אֶחָד **in one day,**

בִּשְׁלֹשָׁה עָשָׂר **on the thirteenth day**

לְחֹדֶשׁ שְׁנֵים עָשָׂר **of the twelfth month**

הוּא חֹדֶשׁ אֲדָר **which is the month of Adar,**

וּשְׁלָלָם לָבוֹז **and to plunder their possessions.**

Haman's anti-semitic campaigns inflamed the general populace to assist him in his plot.[19]

וְאַתָּה **And You,**

בְּרַחֲמֶיךָ הָרַבִּים **in Your abundant mercy,**

הֵפַרְתָּ אֶת עֲצָתוֹ **nullified his plan,**

וְקִלְקַלְתָּ אֶת מַחֲשַׁבְתּוֹ **foiled his intention,**

as it states, "Hashem annuls the counsel of nations; He disrupts the intention of peoples."[20]

וַהֲשֵׁבוֹתָ לּוֹ גְּמוּלוֹ **and turned his evil plan**

בְּרֹאשׁוֹ **upon his own head.**

וְתָלוּ אוֹתוֹ **And they hanged him**

וְאֶת בָּנָיו **and his sons**

עַל הָעֵץ **on the gallows.**

As we look back over all of our requests, we come to realize the extent of our reliance on Hashem for our physical and spiritual needs. With this clear understanding, we declare:

וְעַל כֻּלָּם יִתְבָּרַךְ **And for all of them, blessed**

וְיִתְרוֹמַם שִׁמְךָ **and exalted be Your Name**

מַלְכֵּנוּ תָּמִיד **our King, continually**

לְעוֹלָם וָעֶד **for ever and ever.**
> For all the things mentioned and for the endless other things not mentioned.

Forgot to say this? See page 136

The following is added between Rosh Hashanah and Yom Kippur

וּכְתֹב לְחַיִּים טוֹבִים **And inscribe for a good life**
כָּל בְּנֵי בְרִיתֶךְ **all the children of Your covenant.**

With the coming of *Mashiach* and the restoration of the *Beis Hamikdash*, the universe will once again operate in total harmony and tranquillity. Hashem will reveal His full glory and all truth will be evident.

וְכֹל הַחַיִּים **And all the living**
יוֹדוּךָ סֶּלָה **will thank You for eternity,**
> With all truth revealed, every living thing will acknowledge You as the sole Power, Creator, Owner, Ruler and Benefactor of all existence that was, is, and will be.[21]

וִיהַלְלוּ אֶת **and they will praise**
שִׁמְךָ בֶּאֱמֶת **Your Name in truth,**
> They will declare You King of all kings and admit that we are the Chosen Nation, Yisrael.[22]

הָאֵל **the Almighty,**
יְשׁוּעָתֵנוּ **Who is our salvation**
וְעֶזְרָתֵנוּ סֶלָה **and our help for eternity.**
> You have been our nation's salvation and help through every generation.[23]

בָּרוּךְ אַתָּה **Blessed are You,**
יהוה **Master of the Universe, Who was, is, and always will be,**

הַטּוֹב שִׁמְךָ **The Virtuous One is Your Name**

וּלְךָ נָאֶה לְהוֹדוֹת **and to You it is fitting to give praise.**

Since all good originates from Hashem, Hashem deserves all of our appreciation.

Amen: *It is true, and I believe with complete faith, that all of the favors are due to Your Name "the Virtuous One," and to You it is befitting to give praise.*[24]

ברכת כהנים **The Priestly Blessing** *PAGE 114*

ଓଃ 19: Prayer for Peace ଧ

Just as the kohanim in the *Beis Hamikdash* concluded their blessing of the people with a request for peace, so too, we conclude the *Shemoneh Esrei* with a request for peace.[1]

שִׂים שָׁלוֹם **Place peace,**

Let there be true unity derived from gentleness and brotherly love, not from worry, fear or suffering, a peace that sets aside differences and creates harmony, tranquillity,[2] and peace of mind. Without peace, everything else in life becomes insignificant[3] and even life itself can seem to have lost purpose. Only Hashem can bring about such a true peace.

טוֹבָה **goodness,**

Supply us with beneficial rainfall, our most important material need.[4]

וּבְרָכָה **and blessing,**

Prosperity.[5]

חֵן וָחֶסֶד **graciousness, lovingkindness,**

וְרַחֲמִים **and mercy**

Mercy, as was mentioned previously (see "with abundant mercy" page 41) is the highest level of Hashem's goodness. Only Hashem's mercy can save us from the catastrophic effect of our sins.[6] We therefore ask Hashem for His entire spectrum of goodness.

עָלֵינוּ **upon us**

Those who stand here before You.[7]

וְעַל כָּל יִשְׂרָאֵל **and upon all of Yisrael,**

עַמֶּךְ **Your Nation.**

בָּרְכֵנוּ אָבִינוּ **Bless us, Our Father,**

כֻּלָּנוּ כְּאֶחָד **all of us as one**

בְּאוֹר פָּנֶיךָ **with the light of Your Countenance.**

Unity exalts our nation to its highest level of greatness (see "And gather us in unity," page 64). Bless us with solidarity and do so with the light that emanates from Your "Countenance," or "Face" — the source[8] of Your most precious gifts.

כִּי בְאוֹר **For with the light**

פָּנֶיךָ **of Your Countenance**

נָתַתָּ לָּנוּ **You have given us,**

יהוה **Master of the Universe, Who was, is, and always will be,**

אֱלֹהֵינוּ **Our God, Source of all powers and abilities**

תּוֹרַת חַיִּים **the Torah of life**

The Torah is the road map for a safe and successful journey through life. Diligence and hard work in the study of Torah and the fulfillment of its commandments, guarantees life. Life, though, does not refer to life in this world, but life beginning in this world and continuing into the next — the World to Come.[9]

וְאַהֲבַת חֶסֶד **and a love of kindness (*chesed*),**

All too often we are quick to judge our fellow man, belittling others for their actions, opinions, or behavior. Repeatedly, the outcome is hurtful and often devastating, with irreversible effects. We fail to recognize and absorb a cardinal principle of life: We were put into this world to emulate Hashem and show kindness to one another, always giving the benefit of the doubt.

True kindness is beneficial, yet because it can require giving up our precious time, money, or both, we are often hesitant to act. We therefore thank Hashem for instilling in us a love of doing kindness.[10]

וּצְדָקָה **and righteousness (*tzedakah*),**

Righteousness is greater than kindness. Kindness, at most, only entails giving up a possible chance to profit, while righteousness entails also a willingness to give up what we already have, as when we give hard-earned income to charity. (It is for this very reason that the root of the Hebrew word for charity, צְדָקָה, is righteousness, צֶדֶק.) The Sages go so far as to say that *tzedakah* saves us from danger and prolongs life, earns pardon for our sins, saves us from the fire of Gehinnom, and brings the Final Redemption closer.[11]

וּבְרָכָה **and blessing,**

By following Hashem's ways, carefully keeping all of His commandments, we receive all of His blessings[12] mentioned in the Torah.[13]

וְרַחֲמִים **and mercy,**
> (see "for Your mercy never ends" page 93).

וְחַיִּים **and life,**
> The gift of life itself.14 For each and every breath we are allowed to take, we should thank Hashem.15

וְשָׁלוֹם **and peace.**

שָׁלוֹם רָב **Abundant peace**
> Peace that sets aside differences and creates harmony.

עַל יִשְׂרָאֵל עַמְּךְ **upon Yisrael Your nation**

תָּשִׂים לְעוֹלָם **place forever,**

כִּי אַתָּה הוּא מֶלֶךְ **for it is You Who is King,**

אָדוֹן לְכָל הַשָּׁלוֹם **Master of all peace.**
> Only Hashem can bring about such a true peace.

וְטוֹב בְּעֵינֶיךְ **And may it be good in Your eyes**

לְבָרֵךְ אֶת עַמְּךְ **to bless Your nation**

יִשְׂרָאֵל **Yisrael**

בְּכָל עֵת וּבְכָל שָׁעָה **at all times and at all hours**

בִּשְׁלוֹמֶךְ **with Your peace.**

The following is added between Rosh Hashanah and Yom Kippur

בְּסֵפֶר חַיִּים **In the Book of Life — the book of**

בְּרָכָה וְשָׁלוֹם **blessing and peace,**

וּפַרְנָסָה טוֹבָה **and prosperous income,**

Forgot to say this? See page 137

נִזָּכֵר may we be remembered

וְנִכָּתֵב לְפָנֶיךָ and inscribed before You

אֲנַחְנוּ וְכָל עַמְּךָ we and all Your nation

בֵּית יִשְׂרָאֵל the House of Yisrael

לְחַיִּים טוֹבִים וּלְשָׁלוֹם for a good life and peace.

בָּרוּךְ אַתָּה Blessed are You,

יהוה Master of the world, Who was, is, and always will be,

עֹשֶׂה הַשָּׁלוֹם Maker of the peace

הַמְבָרֵךְ Who blesses

אֶת עַמּוֹ יִשְׂרָאֵל His people Yisrael

בַּשָּׁלוֹם with peace.

Amen: *It is true, and I believe with complete faith, that it is Your attribute to bless Yisrael with peace. May it be Your will to bless us with peace.*[16]

We end the Shemoneh Esrei with the following request:

יִהְיוּ לְרָצוֹן May they be acceptable

אִמְרֵי פִי the expressions of my mouth,

וְהֶגְיוֹן לִבִּי and the thoughts of my heart,
Any sincere gesture begins from the heart.[17]

לְפָנֶיךָ before You,

יהוה Master of the Universe, Who was, is, and always will be,

צוּרִי my Rock
> (See "Rock of our lives," page 91.)

וְגוֹאֲלִי and my Redeemer.
> (See "Savior," page 38 and "Shield of our salvation," page 91.)

As we part from the *Shemoneh Esrei*, we take with us a greater understanding of Hashem and of the never-ending role He plays in our life. We have opened ourselves to many fundamental concepts and values of Judaism, and have deepened our insights into people and the world around us. We take with us a more serious attitude toward our obligation to serve Hashem and to adhere to His mitzvos. All of this provokes the evil inclination, whose whole desire is to stop our progress and drag us back down. We therefore add one final personalized plea before leaving Hashem's presence: We ask that Hashem assist us[18] in subduing our evil inclination, so that our spiritual growth will not be hindered.[19]

אֱלֹהַי My God, Source of all powers and abilities,

נְצֹר לְשׁוֹנִי מֵרָע guard my tongue from evil

וּשְׂפָתַי and my lips

מִדַּבֵּר מִרְמָה from speaking deceitfully.
> Help me protect myself from negative habits of speech[20] such as ridicule, gossip, revealing secrets, backbiting, embarrassing others, causing hatred, lying, cheating, cursing, using unclean language, and the like, so that my mouth may serve You in a positive manner. (Of course, Hashem expects us to take the first step. Logically that step should be to learn the rules of proper speech.)[21] When

we do so, Hashem will reward us with life in the World to Come and treasured days of this world to take there with us.[22]

וְלִמְקַלְלַי **And to those who curse me,**

נַפְשִׁי תִדֹּם **let my soul be silent,**

Hashem treats us as we treat others, measure for measure. If we forego our pride when we are verbally assaulted and neither take it to heart nor lash out in retaliation, Hashem will likewise forego His anger and will treat us mercifully even when we deserve otherwise.[23]

וְנַפְשִׁי כֶּעָפָר לַכֹּל תִּהְיֶה **and let my soul be like dust to all.**

Not responding to insult is very difficult and takes a great deal of self-control. Training oneself to be humble is the key to success. We must always remember: from earth we were created and to earth we will return. Even though soil plays a major role in everyone's existence, it humbles itself under everyone and everything.[24] Humility is the most basic of all good character traits and the most essential. If we humble ourselves before our fellow man, we will earn the respect of everyone.

פְּתַח לִבִּי בְּתוֹרָתֶךָ **Open my heart to Your Torah,**

Hashem, help me break through the barriers blocking my heart from learning Torah, and help me gain greater insight and understanding into Your Torah.

וּבְמִצְוֹתֶיךָ תִּרְדֹּף נַפְשִׁי **and let my soul pursue Your mitzvos.**

What is the purpose of studying Torah if not to fulfill its directives! Therefore, Hashem, instill within me a driving inspiration to do your mitzvos with zest and great desire[25] — not merely out of habit.

וְכָל הַחוֹשְׁבִים עָלַי רָעָה **As for all those who devise evil against me,**

Whether it be spiritual or physical.

מְהֵרָה הָפֵר עֲצָתָם **quickly nullify their plan**

וְקַלְקֵל מַחֲשַׁבְתָּם **and foil their intentions.**

(Optional Prayer)

יְהִי רָצוֹן מִלְּפָנֶיךָ **May it be Your will,**

יהוה **Master of the Universe, Who was, is, and always will be,**

אֱלֹהַי **my God, Source of all power and abilities,**

וֵאלֹהֵי אֲבוֹתַי **and the God of my Forefathers,**

שֶׁלֹּא תַעֲלֶה קִנְאַת אָדָם עָלַי **that no one's jealousy descend upon me**

וְלֹא קִנְאָתִי עַל אֲחֵרִים **nor my jealousy upon others.**

וְשֶׁלֹּא אֶכְעוֹס הַיּוֹם **May I not become angry today**

וְשֶׁלֹּא אַכְעִיסֶךָ **and may I not anger You.**

וְתַצִּילֵנִי **And rescue me**

מִיֵּצֶר הָרָע **from the Evil Inclination**

וְתֵן בְּלִבִּי and place in my heart

הַכְנָעָה וַעֲנָוָה submissiveness and humility.

מַלְכֵּנוּ וֵאלֹהֵינוּ Our King and our God, Source of all powers and abilities,

יַחֵד שִׁמְךָ בְּעוֹלָמֶךָ unify Your Name in Your world,

בְּנֵה עִירְךָ build Your city,

יַסֵּד lay the foundation

בֵּיתֶךָ of Your House,

וְשַׁכְלֵל הֵיכָלֶךָ perfect Your Sanctuary,

וְקַבֵּץ קִבּוּץ גָּלֻיּוֹת gather the dispersed exiles,

וּפְדֵה צֹאנֶךָ redeem Your flock,

וְשַׂמַּח עֲדָתֶךָ and delight Your congregation.

Since we constantly yearn for the Final Redemption, we end our personal supplication with this request:

עֲשֵׂה לְמַעַן שְׁמֶךָ **Act for the sake of Your Name;**
Bring the Final Redemption for the sake of Your Name, so that it will no longer be ridiculed and disgraced[26] (see "for the sake of His Name" page 37).

עֲשֵׂה לְמַעַן יְמִינֶךָ **act for the sake of Your right hand;**
Hashem's left hand guides the natural causes and His right hand guides the supernatural causes.[27] Bring the Redemption for the sake of all the supernatural acts You caused on our behalf.

עֲשֵׂה לְמַעַן קְדֻשָּׁתֶךָ **act for the sake of Your sanctity;**
> For the sake of Your sanctity, bring the Redemption and rebuild the *Beis Hamikdash*, so that You may once again dwell in Your palace crowned in Your holiness.

עֲשֵׂה לְמַעַן תּוֹרָתֶךָ **act for the sake of Your Torah;**
> Without the Final Redemption, the purpose of the Torah will be unfulfilled. Therefore, bring the redemption for the sake of the Torah.

לְמַעַן יֵחָלְצוּן יְדִידֶיךָ **So that Your loved ones may be rescued,**

הוֹשִׁיעָה יְמִינְךָ **let Your right Hand save**

וַעֲנֵנִי **and answer me.**

See page 125 for instructions

יִהְיוּ לְרָצוֹן **May they be acceptable**

אִמְרֵי פִי **the expressions of my mouth**

וְהֶגְיוֹן לִבִּי **and the thoughts of my heart**
> Any sincere gesture starts with the heart.

לְפָנֶיךָ **before You,**

יהוה **Master of the Universe, Who was, is, and always will be,**

צוּרִי **my Rock**

וְגוֹאֲלִי **and my Redeemer.**

As we leave the presence of the Kings of kings, we bow taking three steps backwards and return to the domain of our everyday life.

Turning to the left :

	(Between Rosh Hashanah and Yom Kippur)

עֹשֶׂה שָׁלוֹם בִּמְרוֹמָיו
He Who makes peace in His heavens,
Hashem Who unified fire and water to create the heavens.

עֹשֶׂה הַשָּׁלוֹם בִּמְרוֹמָיו
He Who makes the peace in His heavens,
Hashem Who unified fire and water to create the heavens.

Forgot to say this? See page 138

Turning to the right:

הוּא יַעֲשֶׂה
שָׁלוֹם עָלֵינוּ **may He make peace upon us**

Bowing forwards:

וְעַל כָּל יִשְׂרָאֵל **and upon all Yisrael,**

Returning upright:

וְאִמְרוּ אָמֵן **and say Amen.**

The heavenly angels did not want mankind to receive the Torah,[28] since human beings are susceptible to corruption and sin. Instead, they wanted the Torah for themselves. Our continual exile supports their allegations of our shortcomings. The angels, being adversaries in a way, are ordered to respond to our prayers with "Amen," a declaration of affirmation to all of our needs and requests, and a commitment to assist our supplications in reaching the holiest of places, where we hope they will be fulfilled. [29]

יְהִי רָצוֹן מִלְפָנֶיךָ **May it be Your will**

יְהוָֹה **Master of the Universe, Who was, is, and always will be,**

אֱלֹהֵינוּ **Our God, Source of all powers and abilities,**

וֵאלֹהֵי אֲבוֹתֵינוּ **and the God of our Forefathers,**

שֶׁיִּבָּנֶה בֵּית הַמִּקְדָּשׁ **that the *Beis Hamikdash* be rebuilt**

בִּמְהֵרָה בְיָמֵינוּ **speedily in our days,**

וְתֵן חֶלְקֵנוּ **and grant us our share**

בְּתוֹרָתֶךָ **in Your Torah**

וְשָׁם נַעֲבָדְךָ **and there we will serve You**

בְּיִרְאָה **with reverence**

כִּימֵי עוֹלָם **as in days of old**

וּכְשָׁנִים קַדְמֹנִיּוֹת **and as in earlier years.**

וְעָרְבָה **And let it be pleasing**

לַיהוָֹה **to the Master of the Universe, Who was, is, and always will be,**

מִנְחַת יְהוּדָה **the offering of Yehudah**

וִירוּשָׁלָםִ **and Yerushalayim**

כִּימֵי עוֹלָם **as in the days of old**

וּכְשָׁנִים קַדְמֹנִיּוֹת **and in earlier years.**

And then the sacrifices of the *Beis Hamikdash* in the holy city of Yerushalayim will be restored and again be pleasing to Hashem, just as they once were in the glorious days of yesteryear.

ଔ ברכת כהנים   The Priestly Blessing ଘ

Jews wander the world far and near just to receive blessings from the great sages of their generation. Yet can the blessing of even the greatest sage have a more powerful effect than one given directly by our Creator? The Priestly Benediction is transmitted directly from Hashem and covers all possible physical and spiritual needs we might have. Hashem's ability is unlimited, therefore His blessings are unlimited. However, only true belief in He Who can bring about those blessings will open the door to their fulfillment. True belief can change wishes into reality.

אֱלֹהֵינוּ	**Our God, Source of all powers and abilities,**
וֵאלֹהֵי אֲבוֹתֵינוּ	**and the God of our Forefathers,**
בָּרְכֵנוּ בַּבְּרָכָה	
הַמְשֻׁלֶּשֶׁת בַּתּוֹרָה	**bless us with the threefold blessing in the Torah,**
הַכְּתוּבָה עַל יְדֵי	**written by the hand of**
מֹשֶׁה עַבְדֶּךָ	**Moshe Your servant,**
הָאֲמוּרָה מִפִּי	**pronounced from the mouths of**
אַהֲרֹן וּבָנָיו	**Aharon and his sons,**
כֹּהֲנִים עַם קְדוֹשֶׁךָ	**the Kohanim, Your holy people,**
כָּאָמוּר	**as it is said:**

בָּרוּךְ אַתָּה	**Blessed are You,**
יהוה	**Master of the Universe, Who was, is, and always will be,**
אֱלֹהֵינוּ	**our God, Source of all powers and abilities,**
מֶלֶךְ הָעוֹלָם	**King of the Universe,**

אֲשֶׁר קִדְּשָׁנוּ **Who sanctified us**

בִּקְדֻשָּׁתוֹ שֶׁל אַהֲרֹן **with the holiness of Aharon**

וְצִוָּנוּ **and commanded us**

לְבָרֵךְ אֶת עַמּוֹ **to bless His people**

יִשְׂרָאֵל **Yisrael**

בְּאַהֲבָה **with love.**

Amen: *It is true, and I believe with complete faith, that You sanctified the descendants of Aharon with priesthood and commanded them to bless us — Your people.*

יְבָרֶכְךָ יהוה **May the Master of the Universe, Who was, is, and always will be, bless you**

May Hashem bless you with long life,[1] children,[2] wealth[3] and all the other blessings mentioned in the Torah.[4]

וְיִשְׁמְרֶךָ **and safeguard you.**

May Hashem safeguard you and your belongings from loss and attack.[5] May Hashem guard you from the negative effects of *ayin hara*,[6] the "evil eye," and help you grow spiritually by protecting you from the evil inclination.[7]

יָאֵר יהוה **May the Master of the Universe, Who was, is, and always will be, illuminate**

פָּנָיו **His Face**

אֵלֶיךָ **upon you**

May Hashem enlighten you with spiritual growth and with the inner truth of the Torah.[8] May He grant you children who will grow to become Torah scholars.[9]

וִיחֻנֶּךָּ **and be gracious unto you.**

May you find favor in His eyes and in the eyes of others. May you be graced with His radiance, and may you be graced with affection for Torah study and a Torah life.[10]

יִשָּׂא יהוה **May the Master of the Universe, Who was, is, and always will be, turn**

פָּנָיו **His Face**

אֵלֶיךָ **towards you**

May Hashem suppress His anger,[11] even if you are not deserving. And may He nullify any harmful judgment decreed upon you.[12]

וְיָשֵׂם **and place**

לְךָ **for you**

שָׁלוֹם **peace.**

May Hashem grant you a peaceful life and peace of mind.[13]

אַדִּיר בַּמָּרוֹם **Mighty One on high**

שׁוֹכֵן בִּגְבוּרָה **Who dwells in power,**

אַתָּה שָׁלוֹם **You are peace**

וְשִׁמְךָ שָׁלוֹם **and your Name is Peace.**

יְהִי רָצוֹן **May it be Your will**

שֶׁתָּשִׂים עָלֵינוּ **to place upon us**

וְעַל כָּל עַמְּךָ **and upon Your entire nation**

בֵּית יִשְׂרָאֵל **the House of Yisrael,**

חַיִּים וּבְרָכָה **life and blessing**

לְמִשְׁמֶרֶת שָׁלוֹם **for the preservation of peace.**

(DON'T FORGET TO THANK THE KOHAIN / KOHANIM)

CONTINUE WITH

שִׂים שָׁלוֹם **Place peace.**

ON PAGE 102

TIPS FOR PRAYER

Tips for prayer

DO set regular times for prayer. It will help you remember to pray.

AVOID rushing into prayer. Allow yourself some time beforehand to relax and clear your mind so that you will be able to center your attention on praying respectfully before Hashem.

AVOID coming late to minyan. Coming late means rushing to catch up.

DO pray with a siddur. Focusing on the words inside will help you concentrate on their meaning and keep you from being distracted.

AVOID praying in a minyan where you must pray quickly in order to keep up.

DO pray in a quiet place where you will not be disturbed by talking or noise.

AVOID scheduling activities right after praying, since it will distract you and interfere with your prayers.

DO get to bed early. It is easier to pray with proper concentration when you are well rested.

(To find out more about how to pray, see the *Mishnah Berurah*. Also recommended is *Priority in Prayer* by Rabbi Yisroel Feinhandler, Feldheim Publishers).

NAMES

Names

It is quoted in the name of the *Sh'lah* that it is beneficial to say daily, before the second יהיו לרצון at the end of the *Shemoneh Esrei* (page 111), a verse from Scriptures that either begins with the first letter of our proper Hebrew name(s) and ends with the last letter of the name(s); or, a verse that contains our name (first and middle names only, not family name). This is so as not to forget our Hebrew name when we are asked for it on the Day of Judgment (may we live to 120 years). Rashi notes that anyone who recites the verse for their name daily will be spared the suffering of Gehinnom. Use the list below to locate the verse(s) for your name and write it (them) on the lines provided on page 111.

verse chapter		verse chapter	
ב...ז	תהלים Ps. 138/3	א...א	תהלים Ps. 118/25
ב...ך	תהלים Ps. 119/12	א...ה	תהלים Ps. 41/2
ב...ל	תהלים Ps. 68/27	א...ו	תהלים Ps. 146/5
ב...ן	תהלים Ps. 41/14	א...י	תהלים Ps. 5/2
ב...ע	משלי Prov. 16/6	א...ך	תהלים Ps. 16/2
ג...ד	תהלים Ps. 9/6	א...ל	תהלים Ps. 68/9
ג...ה	תהלים Ps. 37/5	א...ם	נחמיה Neh. 9/7
ג...ל	תהלים Ps. 71/22	א...ן	תהלים Ps. 30/9
ג...ן	תהלים Ps. 49/3	א...ע	תהלים Ps. 10/6
ד...ב	ישעיה Is. 55/6	א...ר	תהלים Ps. 20/8
ד...ד	תהלים Ps. 105/4	ב...א	מלאכי Mal. 2/5
ד...ה	משלי Prov. 12/25	ב...ה	תהלים Ps. 105/45

verse chapter		verse chapter	
Ps. 146/9 תהלים	י...ת	Gen. 49/16 בראשית	ד...ל
Ps. 94/14 תהלים	כ...ב	Deut. 32/4 דברים	ה...א
Ps. 47/8 תהלים	כ...ל	Ps. 51/11 תהלים	ה...ה
Ex. 23/26 שמות	ל...א	Ps. 5/3 תהלים	ה...ל
Ps. 144/1 תהלים	ל...ה	Prov. 10/7 משלי	ז...ב
Ps. 119/92 תהלים	ל...י	Ps. 132/14 תהלים	ז...ה
Ps. 45/1 תהלים	ל...ת	Ps. 143/5 תהלים	ז...ח
Ex. 15/11 שמות	מ...א	Gen. 49/13 בראשית	ז...ן
Prov. 20/18 משלי	מ...ה	Prov. 31/17 משלי	ח...ה
Cant. 5/9 שיר השירים	מ...ו	Ps. 119/62 תהלים	ח...ך
Prov. 15/4 משלי	מ...ח	Ps. 34/8 תהלים	ח...ם
Ps. 119/97 תהלים	מ...י	Prov. 13/22 משלי	ט...א
Num. 24/5 במדבר	מ...ל	Ps. 140/6 תהלים	ט...ה
Prov. 15/30 משלי	מ...ם	Ps. 115/9 תהלים	י...א
Ps. 25/12 תהלים	מ...ר	Ps. 20/2 תהלים	י...ב
Ps. 33/20 תהלים	נ...א	Ps. 104/5 תהלים	י...ד
Ps. 119/111 תהלים	נ...ה	Ps. 120/2 תהלים	י...ה
Ps. 119/108 תהלים	נ...י	Ps. 118/7 תהלים	י...י
Ps. 88/5 תהלים	נ...ל	Ps. 118/16 תהלים	י...ל
Is. 40/1 ישעיה	נ...ם	Ps. 149/5 תהלים	י...ם
Prov. 20/27 משלי	נ...ן	Ps. 107/33 תהלים	י...ן
Ps. 48/13 תהלים	ס...ה	Ps. 72/13 תהלים	י...ע
Ps. 119/113 תהלים	ס...י	Ps. 138/8 תהלים	י...ף
Is. 33/10 ישעיה	ע...א	Ps. 67/8 תהלים	י...ץ
Ps. 132/5 תהלים	ע...ב	Ps. 107/14 תהלים	י...ק
Ps. 118/14 תהלים	ע...ה	Ps. 135/13 תהלים	י...ר

verse chapter		verse chapter	
ר...ל	דברים Deut. 32/39	ע...ל	איוב Job 10/7
ר...ם	משלי Prov. 19/21	ע...ם	תהלים Ps. 119/122
ר...ן	קהלת Eccl. 7/27	ע...ר	איוב Job 5/9
ש...א	תהלים Ps. 86/4	פ...ה	תהלים Ps. 118/19
ש...ה	תהלים Ps. 119/165	פ...ל	תהלים Ps. 7/3
ש...ח	תהלים Ps. 6/10	פ...ס	משלי Prov. 16/11
ש...י	תהלים Ps. 31/7	פ...ץ	תהלים Ps. 80/10
ש...ל	תהלים Ps. 119/165	צ...ה	ישעיה Job 1/27
ש...ם	תהלים Ps. 37/37	צ...ח	ירמיה Jer. 50/5
ש...ן	תהלים Ps. 48/14	צ...י	תהלים Ps. 119/143
ש...ר	משלי Prov. 12/19	צ...ן	שיר השירים Cant. 1/3
ש...ת	תהלים Ps. 134/1	צ...ק	תהלים Ps. 119/138
ת...ה	תהלים Ps. 23/5	ק...ל	שיר השירים Cant. 5/5
ת...י	תהלים Ps. 31/5	ק...ן	תהלים Ps. 142/2
ת...ם	תהלים Ps. 68/35	ק...ת	תהלים Ps. 119/151
		ר...ה	תהלים Ps. 5/4

GUIDELINES FOR CORRECTING MISTAKES IN PRAYER

Guidelines for Correcting Mistakes in Prayer

Our prayers have special insertions at certain times of the year. Since human error sometimes leads us to omit these important additions, we have been given guidelines for correcting our mistakes. Sometimes, we are to stop, return to a previous point in our prayers, and begin from there; at other times, we should continue from where we are and try harder to remember the next time. Presented here are some basic directives on how to proceed in case of omission.

זכרנו לחיים

During the Ten Days of Repentance from Rosh Hashanah to Yom Kippur, there are special additions.

If you forgot to say זכרנו לחיים and realized your omission before saying Hashem's Name in ברוך אתה ה' מגן אברהם (i.e., you only said בָּרוּךְ אַתָּה), stop and go back to זכרנו לחיים:

For example:

מֶלֶךְ עוֹזֵר וּמוֹשִׁיעַ וּמָגֵן. בָּרוּךְ אַתָּה
(OOPS!)
זָכְרֵנוּ לְחַיִּים מֶלֶךְ חָפֵץ בַּחַיִּים...

If, though, you have already said Hashem's Name, continue your prayer without going back to correct the omission.

For example:

מֶלֶךְ עוֹזֵר וּמוֹשִׁיעַ וּמָגֵן. בָּרוּךְ אַתָּה ה'
(OOPS!)
מָגֵן אַבְרָהָם.

מִי כָמוֹךְ

If you forgot to say מִי כָמוֹךְ אַב הרחמים and remembered your omission before saying Hashem's Name in בָּרוּךְ אתה ה' (i.e., you only said בָּרוּךְ אַתָּה), stop and go back to מִי כָמוֹךְ אַב הרחמים.

For example:

וְנֶאֱמָן אַתָּה לְהַחֲיוֹת מֵתִים. בָּרוּךְ אַתָּה
(OOPS!)
מִי כָמוֹךְ אַב הָרַחֲמִים...

If, though, you have already said Hashem's Name, continue your prayer as usual, without going back to correct the omission.

For example:

בָּרוּךְ אַתָּה ה'
(OOPS!)
מְחַיֵּה הַמֵּתִים.

הַמֶּלֶךְ הַקָּדוֹשׁ

If instead of saying הַמֶּלֶךְ הַקָּדוֹשׁ you said the usual הָקֵל
הַקָּדוֹשׁ, but remembered immediately before starting the next
blessing אַתָּה חוֹנֵן, say without hesitation* הַמֶּלֶךְ הַקָּדוֹשׁ.

For example:

בָּרוּךְ אַתָּה ה' הָקֵל הַקָּדוֹשׁ
(OOPS!)
הַמֶּלֶךְ הַקָּדוֹשׁ.

If, though, you hesitated*, or started saying the next blessing
אַתָּה חוֹנֵן, you must go back to the beginning of the
Shemoneh Esrei (starting from בָּרוּךְ אַתָּה ה'...).

During the rest of the year, if you mistakenly said הַמֶּלֶךְ
הַקָּדוֹשׁ instead of הָקֵל הַקָּדוֹשׁ, you do not go back.

---

* Hesitation is defined as being the length of time it takes to say "Shalom
alechah rebbe."

הַמֶּלֶךְ הַמִּשְׁפָּט

If instead of saying הַמֶּלֶךְ הַמִּשְׁפָּט you said the usual מֶלֶךְ אוֹהֵב צְדָקָה וּמִשְׁפָּט, but remembered immediately before starting the next blessing וְלַמַּלְשִׁינִים, say without hesitation* הַמֶּלֶךְ הַמִּשְׁפָּט.

For example:

בָּרוּךְ אַתָּה ה' מֶלֶךְ אוֹהֵב צְדָקָה וּמִשְׁפָּט
(OOPS!)
הַמִּשְׁפָּט הַמֶּלֶךְ.

If, though, you hesitated,* or started saying the next blessing וְלַמַּלְשִׁינִים, continue as usual.

---

* Hesitation is defined as being the length of time it takes to say "Shalom alechah rebbe."

וכתוב לחיים

If you forgot to say וכתוב לחיים, but remembered your omission before saying Hashem's Name in ברוך אתה ה' הטוב שמך ולך נאה להודות (i.e., you only said בָּרוּךְ אַתָּה), stop and go back to וכתוב לחיים.

For example:

הָקֵל יְשׁוּעָתֵנוּ וְעֶזְרָתֵנוּ סֶלָה. בָּרוּךְ אַתָּה
(OOPS!)
וכְתוֹב לְחַיִּים טוֹבִים כָּל בְּנֵי בְרִיתֶךָ. וְכָל הַחַיִּים...

If, though, you have already said Hashem's Name, continue your prayer without going back to correct the omission.

For example:

בָּרוּךְ אַתָּה ה'
(OOPS!)
הַטּוֹב שִׁמְךָ וּלְךָ נָאֶה לְהוֹדוֹת.

בְּסֵפֶר חַיִּים

If you forgot to say בְּסֵפֶר חַיִּים, but remembered your omission before saying Hashem's Name in בְּרוּךְ אַתָּה ה' (i.e., you only said בְּרוּךְ אַתָּה), stop and go back to בְּסֵפֶר חַיִּים.

For example:

בְּכָל עֵת וּבְכָל שָׁעָה בִּשְׁלוֹמֶךָ. בָּרוּךְ אַתָּה...
(OOPS!)
בְּסֵפֶר חַיִּים...

If, though, you already said Hashem's Name, continue your prayer without going back to correct the omission בְּסֵפֶר חַיִּים.

For Example:

בָּרוּךְ אַתָּה ה'
(OOPS!)
הַמְבָרֵךְ אֶת עַמּוֹ בַּשָׁלוֹם.

השלום

If instead of saying עֹשֶׂה הַשָּׁלוֹם, you said the usual עֹשֶׂה שָׁלוֹם, continue as usual.

מַשִּׁיב הָרוּחַ

Rain and dew are essential for all life. We offer heartfelt prayers appropriate to each season imploring Hashem to bestow these blessings upon the world.

The "rainy season" begins from the recitation of *Tefillas HaGeshem* (Prayer for Rain) on *Shemini Atzeres*[1] at the end of *Succos*. It continues throughout the winter until the first day of *Pesach*, when *Tefillas HaTal* (Prayer for Dew) is recited. During these months, מַשִּׁיב הָרוּחַ וּמוֹרִיד הַגֶּשֶׁם is said.

The "dry season" begins from the recitation of *Tefillas HaTal*, and continues throughout the summer until *Tefillas HaGeshem*. is recited.

If you said מַשִּׁיב הָרוּחַ וּמוֹרִיד הַגֶּשֶׁם during the dry season and realized your mistake before saying Hashem's Name, go back to אַתָּה גִבּוֹר and continue as usual.

For example:

וְנֶאֱמָן אַתָּה לְהַחֲיוֹת מֵתִים. בָּרוּךְ אַתָּה
(OOPS!)
אַתָּה גִּבּוֹר...

If, though, you have already said Hashem's Name before realizing your omission, say לַמְּדֵנִי חֻקֶּיךָ and then go back to אַתָּה גיבור, continuing as usual.

1: In many communities it is customary to announce "מַשִּׁיב הָרוּחַ וּמוֹרִיד הַגֶּשֶׁם" prior to *Mussaf* of *Shemini Atzeres*, in which case you should begin reciting מַשִּׁיב הָרוּחַ וּמוֹרִיד הַגֶּשֶׁם after the announcement.

For example:

בָּרוּךְ אַתָּה ה'
(OOPS!)
לַמְּדֵנִי חֻקֶּיךָ. אַתָּה גִבּוֹר...

If, though, you already said, בָּרוּךְ אתה ה' מחיה, go back to
the beginning of the *Shemoneh Esrei* (starting from בָּרוּךְ
אתה).

For example:

וְנֶאֱמָן אַתָּה לְהַחֲיוֹת מֵתִים. בָּרוּךְ אַתָּה ה' מְחַיֶּה.
(OOPS!)
בָּרוּךְ אַתָּה ה' אֱלֹקֵינוּ...

During the rainy season, if you forgot to say משיב הרוח
ומוריד הגשם, and realized your mistake before saying ונאמן,
say משיב הרוח ומוריד הגשם and continue אתה להחיות מתים
as usual.

For example:

...סוֹמֵךְ נוֹפְלִים
(OOPS!)
מַשִּׁיב הָרוּחַ וּמוֹרִיד הַגָּשֶׁם... וְרוֹפֵא חוֹלִים וּמַתִּיר אֲסוּרִים

If you already started ונאמן אתה, but have not yet said
Hashem's Name, say משיב הרוח ומוריד הגשם and begin
again from ונאמן אתה.

For example:

וְנֶאֱמָן אַתָּה לְהַחֲיוֹת מֵתִים
(OOPS!)
מַשִּׁיב הָרוּחַ וּמוֹרִיד הַגָּשֶׁם. וְנֶאֱמָן אַתָּה...

If, though, you have already said Hashem's Name before realizing your omission, say לַמְּדֵנִי חֻקֶּיךָ and then go back to מַשִּׁיב הָרוּחַ וּמוֹרִיד הַגֶּשֶׁם, continuing as usual.

For example:

בָּרוּךְ אַתָּה ה'
(OOPS!)

לַמְּדֵנִי חֻקֶּיךָ. מַשִּׁיב הָרוּחַ וּמוֹרִיד הַגֶּשֶׁם מְכַלְכֵּל...

If you completed the blessing and said מְחַיֵּה הַמֵּתִים, but remembered your omission before starting אַתָּה קָדוֹשׁ, say מַשִּׁיב הָרוּחַ and continue with אַתָּה קָדוֹשׁ.

For example:

בָּרוּךְ אַתָּה ה' מְחַיֵּה הַמֵּתִים
(OOPS!)
מַשִּׁיב הָרוּחַ וּמוֹרִיד הַגֶּשֶׁם. אַתָּה קָדוֹשׁ...

If, though, you have already started אַתָּה קָדוֹשׁ you must go back to the beginning of the *Shemoneh Esrei* (starting from בָּרוּךְ אַתָּה).

For example:

בָּרוּךְ אַתָּה ה' מְחַיֵּה הַמֵּתִים. אַתָּה
(OOPS!)
בָּרוּךְ אַתָּה ה' אֱלֹקֵינוּ...

If you said מוֹרִיד הַטָּל instead of מַשִּׁיב הָרוּחַ and have already said בָּרוּךְ אַתָּה ה', continue as usual. If you have not said בָּרוּךְ אַתָּה ה', follow the above rules.

וְתֵן בְּרָכָה

When we ask Hashem to bless the world with a year of prosperity our prayer is specific to the season.

During the dry season[2], if you mistakenly said וְתֵן טַל וּמָטָר לִבְרָכָה instead of the correct וְתֵן בְּרָכָה and have not yet said Hashem's Name in בָּרוּךְ אַתָּה ה' מְבָרֵךְ הַשָּׁנִים (i.e., you only said בָּרוּךְ אַתָּה), start again from בָּרֵךְ עָלֵינוּ.

For example:

בָּרוּךְ אַתָּה
(OOPS!)
בָּרֵךְ עָלֵינוּ...

If, though, you have already said Hashem's Name before realizing your omission, say לַמְּדֵנִי חֻקֶּיךָ and then go back to בָּרֵךְ עָלֵינוּ, continuing as usual.

---

2. Outside of *Eretz Yisrael*, the "dry season" — when וְתֵן בְּרָכָה is said — starts from the beginning of *Chol Hamoed Pesach* and continues until nightfall of December 4th (or 5th, if it is a civil leap year). In *Eretz Yisrael*, the "dry season" begins from *Chol Hamoed Pesach* and continues until the night of the 7th of Cheshvan.

For example:

בָּרוּךְ אַתָּה ה'
(OOPS!)
לַמְּדֵנִי חֻקֶּיךָ בָּרֵךְ עָלֵינוּ...

If you have already completed the blessing but have not yet said the יהיו לרצון which follows אלקי נצור at the end of the *Shemoneh Esrei*, start again from בָּרֵךְ עָלֵינוּ. If you have already completed saying the יהיו לרצון which follows אלקי נצור, then you must repeat the entire *Shemoneh Esrei*.

וְתֵן טַל וּמָטָר

During the rainy season[3], if you forgot to say וְתֵן טַל וּמָטָר לברכה, but have not yet said Hashem's Name in the concluding blessing, go back to וְתֵן טַל וּמָטָר לברכה and continue as usual.

For example:

...וּבָרֵךְ שְׁנָתֵנוּ כַּשָּׁנִים הַטּוֹבוֹת. בָּרוּךְ אַתָּה
(OOPS!)
...וְתֵן טַל וּמָטָר לִבְרָכָה עַל פְּנֵי הָאֲדָמָה...

If, though, you already said Hashem's Name, continue as usual adding וְתֵן טַל וּמָטָר לברכה in שְׁמַע קוֹלֵנוּ just before כִּי אַתָּה שׁוֹמֵעַ תְּפִלַּת.

For example:

שְׁמַע קוֹלֵנוּ...וּמִלְּפָנֶיךָ מַלְכֵּנוּ רֵיקָם אַל תְּשִׁיבֵנוּ, וְתֵן טַל
וּמָטָר לִבְרָכָה. כִּי אַתָּה...

If you completed the blessing of שְׁמַע קוֹלֵנוּ and realized your omission before starting רצה, say וְתֵן טַל וּמָטָר לברכה and continue with רצה.

---

3. Outside of *Eretz Yisrael*, the "rainy season" — when וְתֵן טַל וּמָטָר לברכה is said — starts from nightfall of December 4th (or 5th, if it is a civil leap year) and continues through the winter until *Pesach*. In *Eretz Yisrael*, the "rainy season" begins on the night of the 7th of Cheshvan and lasts until Pesach.

For example:

בָּרוּךְ אַתָּה ה' שׁוֹמֵעַ תְּפִלָּה.
(OOPS!)
וְתֵן טַל וּמָטָר לִבְרָכָה. רְצֵה...

If you are anywhere from starting רצה till the completion of אלקי נצור when you realize your omission, start again from בָּרֵךְ עָלֵינוּ. If, though, you realize your omission after you finish saying the יהיו לרצון which follows אלקי נצור, you must repeat the entire *Shemoneh Esrei*.

נחם

On *Tisha b'Av* we emphasize our anguish over the destruction of *Yerushalayim* and the Holy Temple with the prayer of נחם and hope that Hashem will console.

If you forget to say נחם and have already said Hashem's Name, recite נחם between the paragraphs of רצה and ותחזינה בְּרוּךְ אַתָּה ה' מְנַחֵם) without saying its closing blessing (עֵינֵינוּ ותחזינה עֵינֵינוּ continuing with (צִיּוֹן וּבוֹנֵה יְרוּשָׁלַיִם.

For example:

בָּרוּךְ אַתָּה ה'
(OOPS!)

בּוֹנֵה יְרוּשָׁלַיִם. רְצֵה...עַמֶּךָ. נַחֵם...בְּתוֹכָה. וְתֶחֱזֶינָה
עֵינֵינוּ...

If you already said Hashem's Name, continue as usual without saying נחם.

עננו

The עֲנֵנוּ prayer is recited on fast days to express our distressing predicament and ask Hashem to answer our prayers.

If you forgot to say עֲנֵנוּ, but remembered your omission before saying Hashem's Name in בָּרוּך אתה ה' שומע תפילה (i.e., you only said בָּרוּךְ אַתָּה), go back to where עֲנֵנוּ is to be inserted and continue as usual.

For example:

כִּי אַתָּה שׁוֹמֵעַ תְּפִלַּת עַמְּךָ יִשְׂרָאֵל בְּרַחֲמִים. בָּרוּך אַתָּה
(OOPS!)
עֲנֵנוּ ה' עֲנֵנוּ...וְצוּקָה. כִּי אַתָּה שׁוֹמֵעַ ...

If you already said Hashem's Name, continue as usual, inserting עֲנֵנוּ just before the יהיו לרצון which follows אלקי נצור. If you already said יהיו לרצון, continue without saying עֲנֵנוּ.

יעלה ויבא

The beginning of every Jewish month, *Rosh Chodesh*, is of special significance and is celebrated as a holiday. In the days of the *Beis Hamikdash*, *Rosh Chodesh* was celebrated with special sacrifices. On *Rosh Chodesh*, יעלה ויבא is included in the regular prayer service requesting that this special day be a day of remembrance and deliverance, lovingkindness and mercy, life and peace. יעלה ויבא is also said on all of the Intermediate Days (*Chol Hamoed*) of Pesach and Succos.

If you forgot to say יעלה ויבא on *Rosh Chodesh*, but have not yet said Hashem's Name in ברוך אתה ה' המחזיר שכינתו לציון (i.e., you only said בָּרוּך אַתָּה), stop and go back to יעלה ויבא.

For example:

וְתֶחֱזֶינָה עֵינֵינוּ...בָּרוּך אַתָּה
(OOPS!)
אֱלֹקֵינוּ וֵאלֹקֵי אֲבוֹתֵינוּ...

Note: In the following cases, if you forgot to say יעלה ויבא on *Rosh Chodesh*, during *Ma'ariv*, continue as usual without saying יעלה ויבא; during *Shacharis* or *Minchah*, you need to correct the omission.

If you said Hashem's Name and then realized your omission, say the words לַמְּדֵנִי חֻקֶּיךָ and then go back to יעלה ויבא.

For example:

וְתֶחֱזֶינָה עֵינֵינוּ...בְּרַחֲמִים. בָּרוּךְ אַתָּה ה'
(OOPS!)
לַמְּדֵנִי חֻקֶּיךָ. אֱלֹקֵינוּ וֵאלֹקֵי אֲבוֹתֵינוּ... חַנּוּן וְרַחוּם אָתָּה.
בָּרוּךְ אַתָּה. ה' הַמַּחֲזִיר שְׁכִינָתוֹ לְצִיּוֹן.

If you already completed the blessing, insert יעלה ויבא before starting מודים.

For example:

בָּרוּךְ אַתָּה ה' הַמַּחֲזִיר שְׁכִינָתוֹ לְצִיּוֹן.
(OOPS!)
אֱלֹקֵינוּ וֵאלֹקֵי אֲבוֹתֵינוּ...חַנּוּן וְרַחוּם אַתָּה. מוֹדִים אֲנַחְנוּ...

If you are anywhere from starting רצה till the completion of אלקי נצור, start again from רצה. If, though, you have already completed saying the יהיו לרצון which follows אלקי נצור, you must repeat the entire *Shemoneh Esrei*.

If you forgot to say יעלה ויבא on the Intermediate Days (*Chol Hamoed*) of Pesach and Succos (even during *Ma'ariv*) follow all of the above rules.

עַל הַנִּסִים

עַל הַנִּסִים is a thanksgiving prayer for the miracles Hashem performed on Chanukah and Purim.

If you forgot to say עַל הַנִּסִים, but remembered your omission before saying Hashem's Name in הַטּוֹב שִׁמְךָ וּלְךָ נָאֶה לְהוֹדוֹת, start again from עַל הַנִּסִים.

For example:

הָאֵל יְשׁוּעָתֵנוּ וְעֶזְרָתֵנוּ סֶלָה. בָּרוּךְ אַתָּה
(OOPS!)
עַל הַנִּסִים...וְעַל כֻּלָּם...

If, though, you already said Hashem's Name, insert עַל הַנִּסִים at the end of the *Shemoneh Esrei* (just before the יהיו לְרָצוֹן which follows אלֹקי נצור) with the following prefix:

הָרַחֲמָן הוּא יַעֲשֶׂה לָנוּ נִסִּים וְנִפְלָאוֹת כְּשֵׁם שֶׁעָשִׂיתָ
לַאֲבוֹתֵינוּ בַּיָּמִים הָהֵם בַּזְּמַן הַזֶּה.

continuing with either בִּימֵי מַתִּתְיָהוּ for Chanukah, or בִּימֵי מָרְדְּכַי for Purim.

If you already said the יהיו לְרָצוֹן which follows אלֹקי נצור, do not say עַל הַנִּסִים and do **not** repeat the *Shemoneh Esrei*.

אתה חוננתנו

The אתה חוננתנו prayer is recited at the conclusion of *Shabbos* or *Yom Tov* to distinguish their holiness from the ordinary days of the year.

If you forgot to say אתה חוננתנו and have already said Hashem's Name, continue as usual without saying אתה חוננתנו, since you will be saying or hearing *Havdalah* later.

For example:

וּמְלַמֵּד לֶאֱנוֹשׁ בִּינָה. חָנֵנוּ מֵאִתְּךָ דֵּעָה בִּינָה וְהַשְׂכֵּל. בָּרוּךְ
אַתָּה ה'
(OOPS!)
חוֹנֵן הַדָּעַת.

SOURCES

Sources

Hebrew

Author	Title
ר' דוד בר' יוסף בר' דוד בן אבודרהם	אבודרהם
ר' אליהו לאנדא	אבני אליהו
ר' אהרן יוסף ברזל	אוצר מוסרי חז"ל
ר' יצחק אליהו לנדא	אחרית שלום
ר' ברוך עפשטיין	ברוך שאמר
ר' יעקב ב"ר אשר	בעל הטורים
ר' יצחק אליהו לנדא	דובר שלום
רבנו בחיי	חובות הלבבות
ר' ישראל מאיר הכהן	חפץ חיים על תפילה
ר' אלכסנדר זיסקינד	יסוד ושורש העבודה
ר' יהונתן אייבשיץ	יערות דבש
ר' יהודה הלוי	הכוזרי
ר' ישראל מאיר הכהן	מחני ישראל (כתבי החח")
ר' אליהו דסלר	מכתב מאליהו
ר' אהרן סגל	נהורא השלם
ר' עובדיה ספורנו	סדר היום
ר' שמעון בן יוחאי	ספרי
עבודת הלבבות (סדור) ר' זאב יעבץ	

ר' אריה ליב גורדון	עיון תפילה
ר' שמואל הומינור	עלת תמיד
ר' יעקב עמדין	עמודי שמים
ר' חנוך זונדל	ענף יוסף
ר' חנוך זונדל	עץ יוסף
ר' אברהם משי-זהב	פרד"ס התפילה
ר' יצחק מאלצאן	שיח יצחק
ר' חיים פרידלנדר	שפתי חיים

English
The Hirsch Siddur, Rabbi Samson Rafael Hirsch, (New York: Feldheim Publishers, 1969)

Praise, My Soul, Rabbi Avigdor Miller, (New York: Beis Yisroel of Rugby, 1982)

World of Prayer, Rabbi Elie Munk, translated by Mr. Henry Biberfeld in collaboration with Mr. Leonhard Oschry, (New York: Feldheim Publishers, 1961)

Strive for truth, Rabbi Eliyahu E. Dessler, rendered in English by Aryeh Carmel, (Israel: Feldheim Publishers, 1985)

FOOTNOTES

Footnotes

(1) עלת תמיד

(2) עלת תמיד

(3) עלת תמיד

(4) אבני אליהו, יערות דבש (חלק א' באמצע דרוש א')

1: The Patriarchs

There are two main ways to translate the word: בָּרוּךְ (1:1)

1. *blessing/bless*, derived from the word בְּרָכָה — *blessing*

2. *increase* or *intensify*, derived from the word בְּרֵיכָה — *spring* (flowing water).

According to those who translate it as *blessing / bless*, the connotation is either:

1a. Hashem is the Source of all *blessing*. Everything we have is from Hashem's vast reserve of blessing and good.

1b. We *bless* Hashem. Even though Hashem is perfect and complete (and certainly not in need of our blessings), by blessing Him we express gratitude for all that He does.

According to those who translate it as *spring*, the connotation is that Hashem should increase and intensify His presence in the world through a flowing abundance of blessing and good.

For simplicity, I have chosen to remain with the traditional translation "Blessed are You" without any further commentary.

Praise, My Soul 1090 (1:2)

(1:3) דובר שלום; פרד"ס התפילה (פנים מאירות)

(1:4) Praise, My Soul 1098

(1:5) מכתב מאליהו חלק ב' (לך לך)

(1:6) מכתב מאליהו חלק ב' (לך לך)

(1:7) מכתב מאליהו חלק ב' (לך לך)

(1:8) אבני אליהו (שלש רגלים)

(1:9) אבודרהם; תהלים קמה:ג

(1:10) ע"פ הלשון "נורא" בהפסוקים אלו ופירושם: דברים א:יט (שפתי חכמים); י:יז (ספורנו); תהלים עו:ח (רד"ק), פט:ח (רד"ק), קיא:ט (רד"ק); חבקוק א:ז (רד"ק, מצודת ציון)

(1:11) שיח יצחק; עלת תמיד

(1:12) אבני אליהו (שלש רגלים)

(1:13) עיון תפילה

(1:14) ויקרא כו:מב

(1:15) עץ יוסף

(1:16) יואל ב:יז

(1:17) עיון תפילה

(1:18) יחזקאל יח:לב, לג:יא

(1:19) עלת תמיד; חפץ חיים; יערות דבש (חלק א' דרוש יד)

(1:20) תהלים קמה:יג

(1:21) מכתב מאליהו חלק ד' (תפילה)

(1:22) מכתב מאליהו חלק ד' (תפילה)

(1:23) מכתב מאליהו חלק ד' (תפילה)

(1:24) עץ יוסף

(1:25) טור ושו"ע (קכד:ו)

(1:26) נהורא השלם; רוקח

2: God's Mightiness

(2:1) עיון תפילה

(2:2) הכוזרי (סידור אוצר התפילות)

(2:3) עיון תפילה

(2:4) אבודרהם; עץ יוסף

(2:5) עיון תפילה

(2:6) נדרים ח:ב; פסחים סח:א

(2:7) שמות טו:כו

(2:8) שיח יצחק

(2:9) ״רבות מחשבות בלב איש ועצת ה' היא תקום״ (משלי יט:כא)
ע״פ הגר״א

(2:10) אבודרהם

(2:11) דברים לב:לט

(2:12) עיון תפילה

(2:13) שפתי חיים

(2:14) See "The virtuous One, for your mercy never ends,"
page 93

(2:15) עץ יוסף

(2:16) עמודי שמים

(2:17) נהורא השלם

3: Holiness of God's Name

(3:1) ישעיה ו:ג

(3:2) תרגום יונתן על הפסוק בישעיה ו:ג

(3:3) אבות ו:יא; מכתב מאליהו א'

(3:4) יחזקאל ג:יב

(3:5) עיון תפילה

(3:6) תהלים קמו:י

(3:7) Hirsch Siddur

(3:8) Praise, My Soul 1151

(3:9) ישעיה נז:טו

(3:10) ויקרא יט:ב

(3:11) נהורא השלם

4: Prayer for Insight

(4:1) חובות הלבבות (שער חשבון הנפש פרק ג' פנים כ"א)

(4:2) Praise, My Soul 1162

(4:3) עץ יוסף

(4:4) ויקרא י:י

(4:5) בראשית א:ד

(4:6) ויקרא כ:כו

(4:7) שמות לא:יז

(4:8) Strive For Truth (page 37)

(4:9) סדר היום ; עמודי שמים

(4:10) ב"ח, ט"ז, מג"א (קכד)

(4:11) נהורא השלם; רוקח

5: Prayer for Repentance

(5:1) הכוזרי (סידור אוצר התפילות); סדר היום

(5:2) תהלים קמה:יח; "הפותח יד בתשובה לקבל פושעים וחטאים"
(תפילת תחנונים)

(5:3) "וישם בלבנו אהבתו ויראתו ולעשות רצונו ולעבדו בלבב שלם"
(תפילת ובא לציון)

(4:5) רוקח; ברוך שאמר

(5:5) עץ יוסף; עלת תמיד; יערות דבש (חלק א' באמצע דרוש א')

(6:5) יסוד ושורש העבודה (שער ה' פרק ג'–ה' וכן לכולם)

(7:5) נהורא השלם; רוקח

6: Prayer for Forgiveness

(1:6) סדר היום

(2:6) רוקח; סדר היום; עלת תמיד

(3:6) רוקח; סדר היום; עלת תמיד

(4:6) עיון תפילה; יערות דבש (חלק א' באמצע דרוש א')

(5:6) עלת תמיד

(6:6) עלת תמיד

(7:6) יסוד ושורש העבודה

(8:6) נהורא השלם; רוקח

7: Prayer for Salvation

(1:7) Hirsch Siddur

(2:7) Hirsch Siddur; סדר היום

(3:7) רש"י מגילה יז:ב

(4:7) רוקח; יערות דבש (חלק א' באמצע דרוש א')

(5:7) נהורא השלם; יערות דבש (חלק א' באמצע דרוש א')

8: Prayer for Healing

(1:8) הכוזרי (סידור אוצר התפילות)

(2:8) עלת תמיד

(3:8) עיון תפילה; עץ יוסף; שיח יצחק; ברוך שאמר

(4:8) עלת תמיד

(8:5) עיון תפילה
(8:6) אבני אליהו
(8:7) רוקח; אחרית שלום; ברוך שאמר
(8:8) נהורא השלם; רוקח

9: Prayer for a Year of prosperity

(9:1) עץ יוסף
(9:2) רוקח
(9:3) עץ יוסף
(9:4) אבני אליהו
(9:5) נהורא השלם; רוקח

10: Ingather our People

(10:1) ישעיה כז:יג
(10:2) ישעיה יא:יב
(10:3) רש"י (בראשית יט:ב)
(10:4) אבודרהם; World of Prayer; "ופדה כנאמיך יהודה וישראל"
(צור ישראל)
(10:5) נהורא השלם

11: Restore True Justice

(11:1) עיון תפילה; עלת תמיד; יערות דבש (חלק א' באמצע דרוש
א')
(11:2) סדר היום
(11:3) ישעיה א:כו
(11:4) עלת תמיד
(11:5) אבודרהם

(11:6) אבני אליהו
(11:7) See "The Virtuous One, for Your mercy never ends"
page 93
(11:8) אבודרהם; עץ יוסף
(11:9) נהורא השלם

12: Eradicate the Heretics

(12:1) ברכות י.
(12:2) תהלים קד:לה
(12:3) "הרשעה"–עיון תפילה; ברוך שאמר
(12:4) שמות כג:כב
(12:4) נהורא השלם

13: Have Mercy on the Righteous

(13:1) תהלים עה:יא; מגילה יז:ב
(13:2) עמודי שמים; עץ יוסף
(13:3) עץ יוסף
(13:4) ברוך שאמר
(13:5) פרד"ס התפילה (אמרי נועם)
(13:6) אבני אליהו; ירמיהו יז:ז
(13:7) עץ יוסף
(13:8) נהורא השלם

14: Rebuild the Holy Yerushalayim

(14:1) יסוד ושורש העבודה
(14:2) זכריה ח:ג
(14:3) עיון תפילה; עץ יוסף; ברוך שאמר

Hirsch Siddur (14:4)

רוקח (14:5)

איכה א:ח (14:6)

איכה א:א (14:7)

איכה א:ב (14:8)

ירמיה ד:לא (רדק) (14:9)

רוקח (14:10)

רוקח (14:11)

איכה ד:יא (14:12)

זכריה ב:ט (14:13)

ישעיה נא:ג (14:14)

נהורא השלם (14:15)

15: The Davidic Dynasty

עץ יוסף; פרד״ס התפילה (אר״י ז״ל); יסוד ושורש העבודה; (15:1)
עמודי שמים

מחנה ישראל פרק כ״ה (15:2)

נהורא השלם (15:3)

16: Accept our Prayers

רוקח (16:1)

עיון תפילה (16:2)

עיון תפילה; ברוך שאמר (16:3)

Hirsch Siddur (16:4)

רוקח (16:5)

רוקח (16:6)

(16:7) רוקח
(16:8) יחזקאל סה:כד
(16:9) נהורא השלם

17: Restore the Service of the Beis Hamikdash

(17:1) עיון תפילה; עץ יוסף
(17:2) ברוך שאמר
(17:3) עיון תפילה; ברוך שאמר
(17:4) עיון תפילה
(17:5) אבודרהם
(17:6) פרד"ס התפילה (ספר החיים)
(17:7) שמות לב:ג
(17:8) רוקח
(17:9) תהלים צד:ג
(17:10) משלי ד:ב
(17:11) משלי ג:יח
(17:12) משלי ג:יז
(17:13) פרד"ס התפילה (תהלה ותפארת)
(17:14) תהלים כ:י
(17:15) שמות כב:כו
(17:16) תהלים קכא:א–ב
(17:17) ישעיה ו:יז
(17:18) הכוזרי (סידור אוצר התפילות)
(17:19) סדר היום; נהורא השלם
(17:20) רוקח

18: Prayer of Thankfulness

(18:1) עיון תפילה; יסוד ושורש העבודה; תהלים קמד:טו

(18:2) עץ יוסף

(18:3) עיון תפילה

(18:4) "ומבלעדיך אין לנו מלך גואל ומושיע" (תפילת עזרת אבותינו)

(18:5) עלת תמיד; "עזרת אבותינו אתה הוא מעולם מגן ומושיע לבני בניהם בכל דור ודור" (עזרת אבותינו)

(18:6) עלת תמיד; איוב יב:י

(18:7) אדון עולם

(18:8) יערות דבש (חלק א' באמצע דרוש א')

(18:9) עץ יוסף

(18:10) פרד"ס התפילה (קדושת לוי)

(18:11) עץ יוסף

(18:12) עיון תפילה

(18:13) Praise, My Soul 1319

(18:14) תהלים כה:ה

(18:15) Hirsch Siddur

(18:16) Hirsch Siddur

(18:17) Hirsch Siddur

(18:18) רוקח

(18:19) Hirsch Siddur

(18:20) תהלים לג:י

(18:21) יסוד ושורש העבודה

(18:22) "על כן נקוה לך..." (תפילת עלינו)

(18:23) "והיא שעמדה..." (הגדה של פסח)

(18:23) נהורא השלם

19: Prayer for Peace

(19:1) מגילה יח.

(19:2) עלת תמיד; יערות דבש (חלק א' באמצע דרוש א'); ברוך שאמר

(19:3) עיון תפילה; יערות דבש (חלק א' באמצע דרוש א')

(19:4) תהלים פה:יג (רש"י, רד"ק, אבן עזרא)

(19:5) דברים כח:ח

(19:6)

(19:7) דובר שלום

(19:8) עיון תפילה

(19:9) דברים כב:ז (תרגום יונתן בן עוזיאל ,בעל הטורים); קדושין לט:ב; חולין קמב:ב; דברים ל:יט—כ (תרגום יונתן בן עוזיאל)

(19:10) עבודת הלבבות

(19:11) אוצר מוסרי חז"ל

(19:12) ויקרא כו:ג—יג; דברים כח:א—יד

(19:13) דברים כח:ב

(19:14) Praise, My Soul 1346

(19:15) בראשית רבה פרק יד:ט

(19:16) נהורה שלם

(19:17) תהלים קל:א

(19:18) עץ יוסף; תהלים קכא:ז; "והסר שטן מלפנינו ומאחרינו" (השכיבנו)

(19:19) עץ יוסף; יערות דבש (חלק א' דרוש ב)

אבודרהם (19:20)

חפץ חיים (19:21)

אוצר מוסרי חז״ל (19:22)

פרד״ס התפילה (מהרש״א–ברכות) (19:23)

פרד״ס התפילה (עירין קדישין תנינא) (19:24)

עץ יוסף (19:25)

יסוד ושורש העבודה (19:26)

שיח יצחק (עיין ״עוז בידך״ בתפילת שמונה עשרה לראש (19:27)
השנה)

שבת פח:א (19:28)

עיון תפילה. (19:29)

ברכת כהנים

אבן עזרא (1)

עץ יוסף (2)

ספרי (3)

ספרי (4)

ספרי (5)

עץ יוסף (6)

ספרי (7)

ספרי (8)

עץ יוסף (9)

ספרי (10)

ספרי (11)

ספרי (12)

ספרי (13)

GLOSSARY

Glossary

Aishes Chayil: Woman of Valor

Ashur: Assyria

Beis Hamikdash: The Holy Temple which was situated in Jerusalem

Bereishis: The Book of Genesis

Bitachon: Trust in God

Chanukah: Hanukkah

Chesed: Lovingkindness

Chol HaMoed: Intermediate days of Passover and the Festival of Tabernacles

Dovid (HaMelech): King David

Eichah: Lamentations

Eisav: Esau

Emunah: Belief in God

Gehinnom:

Hashem: God (lit. the Name)

Havdalah: Blessing recited at the closing of the Sabbath

Hoshea: Hosea

Kedushah: Sanctity

Kohain (Kohanim): Priest(s) who served in the Beis Hamikdash; male descendant(s) of Aaron

Ma'ariv: Daily prayer service said after nightfall

Mattisyahu: Mathathias

Minchah: The afternoon prayer service

Mishnah Berurah: A six-volume encyclopedic commentary on the first section of the Shulchan Aruch

Mitzvos: Commandments

Moshe: Moses

Mashiach: Messiah (lit. the anointed one)

Nachas: Joy

Noach: Noah

Pesach: Passover

Pirkei Avos: Ethics of our Fathers

Rosh Chodesh: The monthly holiday celebrating the new moon (lit. the Head of the Month)

Sanhedrin: Supreme Court of Jewish law

Shabbos: The Sabbath

Shacharis: Morning prayer service

Shemoneh Esrei: The Eighteen Benedictions (plus one); also referred to as the Amidah

Shlah: Acronym for SHnei Luchos HaBris written by Rabbi Yesha'yah Horwitz

Shteig: (Yid.) Grow

Shulchan Aruch: The Code of Jewish Law; referred to as the Oral Law

Succos: Succoth or Feast of the Tabernacles

Torah: Pentateuch

Tehillim: Psalms

Tish'ah b'Av: The ninth day of Av; a day of fasting and mourning commemorating the destruction of the first and second Temples

Tzedakah: Charity or Righteousness

Yaakov: Jacob

Yehudah: Judah

Yerushalayim: Jerusalem

Yeshayah: the Prophet Isaiah
Yirmiyahu (or Yirmeyah): the Prophet Jermiah
Yisrael: The people or nation of Israel
Yitzchak: Issac
Yochanan: Yohanan
Yom Tov: Jewish festival

MINCHAH
AND
MA'ARIV

מנחה לחול

וַיְדַבֵּר יְיָ אֶל מֹשֶׁה לֵּאמֹר. וְעָשִׂיתָ כִּיּוֹר נְחֹשֶׁת, וְכַנּוֹ נְחֹשֶׁת, לְרָחְצָה, וְנָתַתָּ אֹתוֹ בֵּין אֹהֶל מוֹעֵד וּבֵין הַמִּזְבֵּחַ, וְנָתַתָּ שָׁמָּה מָיִם. וְרָחֲצוּ אַהֲרֹן וּבָנָיו מִמֶּנּוּ, אֶת יְדֵיהֶם וְאֶת רַגְלֵיהֶם. בְּבֹאָם אֶל אֹהֶל מוֹעֵד יִרְחֲצוּ מַיִם וְלֹא יָמֻתוּ, אוֹ בְגִשְׁתָּם אֶל הַמִּזְבֵּחַ לְשָׁרֵת לְהַקְטִיר אִשֶּׁה לַיְיָ. וְרָחֲצוּ יְדֵיהֶם וְרַגְלֵיהֶם וְלֹא יָמֻתוּ, וְהָיְתָה לָהֶם חָק עוֹלָם, לוֹ וּלְזַרְעוֹ לְדֹרֹתָם.

וַיְדַבֵּר יְיָ אֶל מֹשֶׁה לֵּאמֹר. צַו אֶת אַהֲרֹן וְאֶת בָּנָיו לֵאמֹר, זֹאת תּוֹרַת הָעֹלָה, הִוא הָעֹלָה עַל מוֹקְדָה עַל הַמִּזְבֵּחַ כָּל הַלַּיְלָה עַד הַבֹּקֶר, וְאֵשׁ הַמִּזְבֵּחַ תּוּקַד בּוֹ. וְלָבַשׁ הַכֹּהֵן מִדּוֹ בַד, וּמִכְנְסֵי בַד יִלְבַּשׁ עַל בְּשָׂרוֹ, וְהֵרִים אֶת הַדֶּשֶׁן אֲשֶׁר תֹּאכַל הָאֵשׁ אֶת הָעֹלָה עַל הַמִּזְבֵּחַ, וְשָׂמוֹ אֵצֶל הַמִּזְבֵּחַ. וּפָשַׁט אֶת בְּגָדָיו, וְלָבַשׁ בְּגָדִים אֲחֵרִים, וְהוֹצִיא אֶת הַדֶּשֶׁן אֶל מִחוּץ לַמַּחֲנֶה, אֶל מָקוֹם טָהוֹר. וְהָאֵשׁ עַל הַמִּזְבֵּחַ תּוּקַד בּוֹ, לֹא תִכְבֶּה, וּבִעֵר עָלֶיהָ הַכֹּהֵן עֵצִים בַּבֹּקֶר בַּבֹּקֶר, וְעָרַךְ עָלֶיהָ הָעֹלָה, וְהִקְטִיר עָלֶיהָ חֶלְבֵי הַשְּׁלָמִים. אֵשׁ תָּמִיד תּוּקַד עַל הַמִּזְבֵּחַ, לֹא תִכְבֶּה.

יְהִי רָצוֹן מִלְּפָנֶיךָ, יְיָ אֱלֹהֵינוּ וֵאלֹהֵי אֲבוֹתֵינוּ, שֶׁתְּרַחֵם עָלֵינוּ וְתִמְחָל לָנוּ עַל כָּל חַטֹּאתֵינוּ, וּתְכַפֵּר לָנוּ אֶת כָּל עֲוֹנוֹתֵינוּ, וְתִסְלַח לְכָל פְּשָׁעֵינוּ, וְתִבְנֶה בֵּית הַמִּקְדָּשׁ בִּמְהֵרָה בְיָמֵינוּ, וְנַקְרִיב לְפָנֶיךָ קָרְבַּן הַתָּמִיד שֶׁיְּכַפֵּר בַּעֲדֵנוּ, כְּמוֹ שֶׁכָּתַבְתָּ עָלֵינוּ בְּתוֹרָתֶךְ עַל יְדֵי מֹשֶׁה עַבְדֶּךָ, מִפִּי כְבוֹדֶךָ, כָּאָמוּר:

וַיְדַבֵּר יְיָ אֶל מֹשֶׁה לֵּאמֹר. צַו אֶת בְּנֵי יִשְׂרָאֵל וְאָמַרְתָּ אֲלֵהֶם, אֶת קָרְבָּנִי לַחְמִי לְאִשַּׁי רֵיחַ נִיחֹחִי, תִּשְׁמְרוּ לְהַקְרִיב לִי בְּמוֹעֲדוֹ. וְאָמַרְתָּ לָהֶם, זֶה הָאִשֶּׁה אֲשֶׁר תַּקְרִיבוּ לַיְיָ כְּבָשִׂים בְּנֵי שָׁנָה

תְּמִימִם, שְׁנַיִם לַיּוֹם, עֹלָה תָמִיד. אֶת הַכֶּבֶשׂ אֶחָד תַּעֲשֶׂה בַבֹּקֶר,
וְאֵת הַכֶּבֶשׂ הַשֵּׁנִי תַּעֲשֶׂה בֵּין הָעַרְבָּיִם. וַעֲשִׂירִית הָאֵיפָה סֹלֶת
לְמִנְחָה, בְּלוּלָה בְּשֶׁמֶן כָּתִית רְבִיעִת הַהִין. עֹלַת תָּמִיד, הָעֲשֻׂיָה
בְּהַר סִינַי, לְרֵיחַ נִיחֹחַ אִשֶּׁה לַיְיָ. וְנִסְכּוֹ רְבִיעִת הַהִין לַכֶּבֶשׂ
הָאֶחָד, בַּקֹּדֶשׁ הַסֵּךְ נֶסֶךְ שֵׁכָר לַיְיָ. וְאֵת הַכֶּבֶשׂ הַשֵּׁנִי תַּעֲשֶׂה בֵּין
הָעַרְבָּיִם, כְּמִנְחַת הַבֹּקֶר וּכְנִסְכּוֹ תַּעֲשֶׂה, אִשֵּׁה רֵיחַ נִיחֹחַ לַיְיָ.

וְשָׁחַט אֹתוֹ עַל יֶרֶךְ הַמִּזְבֵּחַ צָפֹנָה לִפְנֵי יְיָ, וְזָרְקוּ בְּנֵי אַהֲרֹן
הַכֹּהֲנִים אֶת דָּמוֹ עַל הַמִּזְבֵּחַ סָבִיב.

יְהִי רָצוֹן מִלְּפָנֶיךָ, יְיָ אֱלֹהֵינוּ וֵאלֹהֵי אֲבוֹתֵינוּ, שֶׁתְּהֵא אֲמִירָה זוֹ
חֲשׁוּבָה וּמְקֻבֶּלֶת וּמְרֻצָּה לְפָנֶיךָ כְּאִלּוּ הִקְרַבְנוּ קָרְבַּן הַתָּמִיד
בְּמוֹעֲדוֹ וּבִמְקוֹמוֹ וּכְהִלְכָתוֹ.

אַתָּה הוּא יְיָ אֱלֹהֵינוּ שֶׁהִקְטִירוּ אֲבוֹתֵינוּ לְפָנֶיךָ אֶת קְטֹרֶת הַסַּמִּים
בִּזְמַן שֶׁבֵּית הַמִּקְדָּשׁ (הָיָה) קַיָּם, כַּאֲשֶׁר צִוִּיתָ אוֹתָם עַל יְדֵי מֹשֶׁה
נְבִיאֶךָ, כַּכָּתוּב בְּתוֹרָתֶךָ:

וַיֹּאמֶר יְיָ אֶל מֹשֶׁה, קַח לְךָ סַמִּים, נָטָף וּשְׁחֵלֶת וְחֶלְבְּנָה, סַמִּים
וּלְבֹנָה זַכָּה, בַּד בְּבַד יִהְיֶה. וְעָשִׂיתָ אֹתָהּ קְטֹרֶת, רֹקַח, מַעֲשֵׂה
רוֹקֵחַ, מְמֻלָּח, טָהוֹר, קֹדֶשׁ. וְשָׁחַקְתָּ מִמֶּנָּה הָדֵק, וְנָתַתָּה מִמֶּנָּה
לִפְנֵי הָעֵדֻת בְּאֹהֶל מוֹעֵד אֲשֶׁר אִוָּעֵד לְךָ שָׁמָּה, קֹדֶשׁ קָדָשִׁים
תִּהְיֶה לָכֶם.

וְנֶאֱמַר: וְהִקְטִיר עָלָיו אַהֲרֹן קְטֹרֶת סַמִּים, בַּבֹּקֶר בַּבֹּקֶר, בְּהֵיטִיבוֹ
אֶת הַנֵּרֹת יַקְטִירֶנָּה. וּבְהַעֲלֹת אַהֲרֹן אֶת הַנֵּרֹת בֵּין הָעַרְבַּיִם,
יַקְטִירֶנָּה, קְטֹרֶת תָּמִיד לִפְנֵי יְיָ לְדֹרֹתֵיכֶם.

תָּנוּ רַבָּנָן, פִּטּוּם הַקְּטֹרֶת כֵּיצַד. שְׁלֹשׁ מֵאוֹת וְשִׁשִּׁים וּשְׁמוֹנָה מָנִים
הָיוּ בָהּ. שְׁלֹשׁ מֵאוֹת וְשִׁשִּׁים וַחֲמִשָּׁה כְּמִנְיַן יְמוֹת הַחַמָּה מָנֶה לְכָל
יוֹם, פְּרָס בְּשַׁחֲרִית וּפְרָס בֵּין הָעַרְבָּיִם, וּשְׁלֹשָׁה מָנִים יְתֵרִים,
שֶׁמֵּהֶם מַכְנִיס כֹּהֵן גָּדוֹל מְלֹא חָפְנָיו בְּיוֹם הַכִּפּוּרִים. וּמַחֲזִירָן
לְמַכְתֶּשֶׁת בְּעֶרֶב יוֹם הַכִּפּוּרִים, וְשׁוֹחֲקָן יָפֶה יָפֶה כְּדֵי שֶׁתְּהֵא דַקָּה

מִן הַדַּקָּה. וְאֶחָד עָשָׂר סַמָּנִים הָיוּ בָהּ, וְאֵלּוּ הֵן: הַצֳּרִי, וְהַצִּפֹּרֶן,
הַחֶלְבְּנָה, וְהַלְּבוֹנָה, מִשְׁקַל שִׁבְעִים שִׁבְעִים מָנֶה: מוֹר, וּקְצִיעָה,
שִׁבֹּלֶת נֵרְדְּ, וְכַרְכֹּם, מִשְׁקַל שִׁשָּׁה עָשָׂר שִׁשָּׁה עָשָׂר מָנֶה: הַקֹּשְׁטְ
שְׁנֵים עָשָׂר, וְקִלּוּפָה שְׁלֹשָׁה, וְקִנָּמוֹן תִּשְׁעָה. בֹּרִית כַּרְשִׁינָה
תִּשְׁעָה קַבִּין, יֵין קַפְרִיסִין סְאִין תְּלָתָא וְקַבִּין תְּלָתָא, וְאִם אֵין לוֹ
יֵין קַפְרִיסִין, מֵבִיא חֲמַר חִוַּרְיָן עַתִּיק, מֶלַח סְדוֹמִית רֹבַע הַקַּב,
מַעֲלֶה עָשָׁן כָּל שֶׁהוּא. רַבִּי נָתָן הַבַּבְלִי אוֹמֵר: אַף כִּפַּת הַיַּרְדֵּן
כָּל שֶׁהוּא. וְאִם נָתַן בָּהּ דְּבַשׁ, פְּסָלָהּ. וְאִם חִסַּר אַחַת מִכָּל
סַמָּנֶיהָ, חַיָּב מִיתָה.

רַבָּן שִׁמְעוֹן בֶּן גַּמְלִיאֵל אוֹמֵר: הַצֳּרִי אֵינוֹ אֶלָּא שְׂרָף הַנּוֹטֵף מֵעֲצֵי
הַקְּטָף. בֹּרִית כַּרְשִׁינָה לָמָּה הִיא בָאָה, כְּדֵי לְיַפּוֹת בָּהּ אֶת
הַצִּפֹּרֶן, כְּדֵי שֶׁתְּהֵא נָאָה. יֵין קַפְרִיסִין לָמָּה הוּא בָא, כְּדֵי לִשְׁרוֹת
בּוֹ אֶת הַצִּפֹּרֶן, כְּדֵי שֶׁתְּהֵא עַזָּה. וַהֲלֹא מֵי רַגְלַיִם יָפִין לָהּ, אֶלָּא
שֶׁאֵין מַכְנִיסִין מֵי רַגְלַיִם בַּמִּקְדָּשׁ מִפְּנֵי הַכָּבוֹד.

תַּנְיָא, רַבִּי נָתָן אוֹמֵר: כְּשֶׁהוּא שׁוֹחֵק, אוֹמֵר הָדֵק הֵיטֵב, הֵיטֵב
הָדֵק, מִפְּנֵי שֶׁהַקּוֹל יָפֶה לַבְּשָׂמִים. פִּטְּמָהּ לַחֲצָאִין, כְּשֵׁרָה:
לִשְׁלִישׁ וְלִרְבִיעַ, לֹא שָׁמָעְנוּ. אָמַר רַבִּי יְהוּדָה: זֶה הַכְּלָל אִם
כְּמִדָּתָהּ, כְּשֵׁרָה לַחֲצָאִין, וְאִם חִסַּר אַחַת מִכָּל סַמָּנֶיהָ, חַיָּב מִיתָה.

תַּנְיָא, בַּר קַפָּרָא אוֹמֵר: אַחַת לְשִׁשִּׁים אוֹ לְשִׁבְעִים שָׁנָה הָיְתָה
בָאָה שֶׁל שִׁירַיִם לַחֲצָאִין. וְעוֹד תָּנֵי בַּר קַפָּרָא: אִלּוּ הָיָה נוֹתֵן בָּהּ
קֹרְטוֹב שֶׁל דְּבַשׁ, אֵין אָדָם יָכוֹל לַעֲמֹד מִפְּנֵי רֵיחָהּ. וְלָמָּה אֵין
מְעָרְבִין בָּהּ דְּבַשׁ, מִפְּנֵי שֶׁהַתּוֹרָה אָמְרָה: כִּי כָל שְׂאֹר וְכָל דְּבַשׁ
לֹא תַקְטִירוּ מִמֶּנּוּ אִשֶּׁה לַיְיָ.

גּ' פְּעָמִים: יְיָ צְבָאוֹת עִמָּנוּ, מִשְׂגָּב לָנוּ אֱלֹהֵי יַעֲקֹב, סֶלָה.

גּ' פְּעָמִים: יְיָ צְבָאוֹת, אַשְׁרֵי אָדָם בֹּטֵחַ בָּךְ.

גּ' פְּעָמִים: יְיָ הוֹשִׁיעָה, הַמֶּלֶךְ יַעֲנֵנוּ בְיוֹם קָרְאֵנוּ.

אַתָּה סֵתֶר לִי, מִצַּר תִּצְּרֵנִי, רָנֵּי פַלֵּט, תְּסוֹבְבֵנִי, סֶלָה. וְעָרְבָה
לַיְיָ מִנְחַת יְהוּדָה וִירוּשָׁלָיִם, כִּימֵי עוֹלָם וּכְשָׁנִים קַדְמֹנִיּוֹת.

אַבַּיֵּי הֲוָה מְסַדֵּר סֵדֶר הַמַּעֲרָכָה מִשְּׁמָא דִגְמָרָא וְאַלִּבָּא דְאַבָּא
שָׁאוּל: מַעֲרָכָה גְדוֹלָה קוֹדֶמֶת לְמַעֲרָכָה שְׁנִיָּה שֶׁל קְטֹרֶת,
וּמַעֲרָכָה שְׁנִיָּה שֶׁל קְטֹרֶת קוֹדֶמֶת לְסִדּוּר שְׁנֵי גִזְרֵי עֵצִים, וְסִדּוּר
שְׁנֵי גִזְרֵי עֵצִים קוֹדֵם לְדִשּׁוּן מִזְבֵּחַ הַפְּנִימִי, וְדִשּׁוּן מִזְבֵּחַ הַפְּנִימִי
קוֹדֵם לַהֲטָבַת חָמֵשׁ נֵרוֹת, וַהֲטָבַת חָמֵשׁ נֵרוֹת קוֹדֶמֶת לְדַם
הַתָּמִיד, וְדַם הַתָּמִיד קוֹדֵם לַהֲטָבַת שְׁתֵּי נֵרוֹת, וַהֲטָבַת שְׁתֵּי נֵרוֹת
קוֹדֶמֶת לִקְטֹרֶת, וּקְטֹרֶת קוֹדֶמֶת לְאֵבָרִים, וְאֵבָרִים לְמִנְחָה,
וּמִנְחָה לַחֲבִתִּין, וַחֲבִתִּין לִנְסָכִין, וּנְסָכִין לְמוּסָפִין, וּמוּסָפִין
לְבָזִיכִין, וּבָזִיכִין קוֹדְמִין לְתָמִיד שֶׁל בֵּין הָעַרְבָּיִם, שֶׁנֶּאֱמַר:
וְעָרַךְ עָלֶיהָ הָעֹלָה, וְהִקְטִיר עָלֶיהָ חֶלְבֵי הַשְּׁלָמִים. עָלֶיהָ הַשְׁלֵם
כָּל הַקָּרְבָּנוֹת כֻּלָּם.

אָנָּא בְּכֹחַ גְּדֻלַּת יְמִינְךָ תַּתִּיר צְרוּרָה. (אב״ג ית״ץ)

קַבֵּל רִנַּת עַמְּךָ שַׂגְּבֵנוּ טַהֲרֵנוּ נוֹרָא. (קר״ע שט״ן)

נָא גִבּוֹר דּוֹרְשֵׁי יִחוּדְךָ כְּבָבַת שָׁמְרֵם. (נג״ד יכ״ש)

בָּרְכֵם טַהֲרֵם רַחֲמֵם צִדְקָתְךָ תָּמִיד גָּמְלֵם. (בט״ר צת״ג)

חֲסִין קָדוֹשׁ בְּרֹב טוּבְךָ נַהֵל עֲדָתֶךָ. (חק״ב טנ״ע)

יָחִיד גֵּאֶה לְעַמְּךָ פְּנֵה זוֹכְרֵי קְדֻשָּׁתֶךָ. (יג״ל פז״ק)

שַׁוְעָתֵנוּ קַבֵּל וּשְׁמַע צַעֲקָתֵנוּ יוֹדֵעַ תַּעֲלוּמוֹת. (שק״ו צי״ת)

בָּרוּךְ שֵׁם כְּבוֹד מַלְכוּתוֹ לְעוֹלָם וָעֶד.

אַשְׁרֵי יוֹשְׁבֵי בֵיתֶךָ, עוֹד יְהַלְלוּךָ סֶּלָה: אַשְׁרֵי הָעָם שֶׁכָּכָה
לוֹ, אַשְׁרֵי הָעָם שֶׁיְיָ אֱלֹהָיו: תְּהִלָּה לְדָוִד, אֲרוֹמִמְךָ אֱלוֹהַי
הַמֶּלֶךְ, וַאֲבָרְכָה שִׁמְךָ לְעוֹלָם וָעֶד: בְּכָל יוֹם אֲבָרְכֶךָ,
וַאֲהַלְלָה שִׁמְךָ לְעוֹלָם וָעֶד: גָּדוֹל יְיָ וּמְהֻלָּל מְאֹד, וְלִגְדֻלָּתוֹ
אֵין חֵקֶר: דּוֹר לְדוֹר יְשַׁבַּח מַעֲשֶׂיךָ, וּגְבוּרֹתֶיךָ יַגִּידוּ: הֲדַר
כְּבוֹד הוֹדֶךָ, וְדִבְרֵי נִפְלְאֹתֶיךָ אָשִׂיחָה: וֶעֱזוּז נוֹרְאוֹתֶיךָ
יֹאמֵרוּ וּגְדֻלָּתְךָ אֲסַפְּרֶנָּה: זֵכֶר רַב טוּבְךָ יַבִּיעוּ, וְצִדְקָתְךָ
יְרַנֵּנוּ: חַנּוּן וְרַחוּם יְיָ, אֶרֶךְ אַפַּיִם וּגְדָל חָסֶד: טוֹב יְיָ לַכֹּל,
וְרַחֲמָיו עַל כָּל מַעֲשָׂיו: יוֹדוּךָ יְיָ כָּל מַעֲשֶׂיךָ, וַחֲסִידֶיךָ
יְבָרְכוּכָה: כְּבוֹד מַלְכוּתְךָ יֹאמֵרוּ, וּגְבוּרָתְךָ יְדַבֵּרוּ: לְהוֹדִיעַ
לִבְנֵי הָאָדָם גְּבוּרֹתָיו, וּכְבוֹד הֲדַר מַלְכוּתוֹ: מַלְכוּתְךָ מַלְכוּת
כָּל עוֹלָמִים, וּמֶמְשַׁלְתְּךָ בְּכָל דֹּר וָדֹר: סוֹמֵךְ יְיָ לְכָל
הַנֹּפְלִים, וְזוֹקֵף לְכָל הַכְּפוּפִים: עֵינֵי כֹל אֵלֶיךָ יְשַׂבֵּרוּ,
וְאַתָּה נוֹתֵן לָהֶם אֶת אָכְלָם בְּעִתּוֹ: פּוֹתֵחַ אֶת יָדֶךָ, וּמַשְׂבִּיעַ
לְכָל חַי רָצוֹן: צַדִּיק יְיָ בְּכָל דְּרָכָיו, וְחָסִיד בְּכָל מַעֲשָׂיו:
קָרוֹב יְיָ לְכָל קֹרְאָיו, לְכֹל אֲשֶׁר יִקְרָאֻהוּ בֶאֱמֶת: רְצוֹן יְרֵאָיו
יַעֲשֶׂה, וְאֶת שַׁוְעָתָם יִשְׁמַע וְיוֹשִׁיעֵם: שׁוֹמֵר יְיָ אֶת כָּל
אֹהֲבָיו, וְאֵת כָּל הָרְשָׁעִים יַשְׁמִיד: תְּהִלַּת יְיָ יְדַבֶּר פִּי, וִיבָרֵךְ
כָּל בָּשָׂר שֵׁם קָדְשׁוֹ, לְעוֹלָם וָעֶד: וַאֲנַחְנוּ נְבָרֵךְ יָהּ, מֵעַתָּה
וְעַד עוֹלָם, הַלְלוּיָהּ:

יִתְגַּדַּל וְיִתְקַדַּשׁ שְׁמֵהּ רַבָּא. בְּעָלְמָא דִּי בְרָא כִרְעוּתֵהּ, וְיַמְלִיךְ
מַלְכוּתֵהּ בְּחַיֵּיכוֹן וּבְיוֹמֵיכוֹן וּבְחַיֵּי דְכָל בֵּית יִשְׂרָאֵל. בַּעֲגָלָא
וּבִזְמַן קָרִיב וְאִמְרוּ אָמֵן:

יְהֵא שְׁמֵהּ רַבָּא מְבָרַךְ לְעָלַם וּלְעָלְמֵי עָלְמַיָּא:

יִתְבָּרַךְ וְיִשְׁתַּבַּח, וְיִתְפָּאַר וְיִתְרוֹמַם וְיִתְנַשֵּׂא וְיִתְהַדָּר וְיִתְעַלֶּה
וְיִתְהַלָּל שְׁמֵהּ דְּקֻדְשָׁא בְּרִיךְ הוּא לְעֵלָּא מִן כָּל (בעשי״ת לְעֵלָּא
וּלְעֵלָּא מִכָּל) בִּרְכָתָא וְשִׁירָתָא, תֻּשְׁבְּחָתָא וְנֶחָמָתָא, דַּאֲמִירָן
בְּעָלְמָא, וְאִמְרוּ אָמֵן:

Shemoneh Esrei (page 33)

אָבִינוּ מַלְכֵּנוּ חָטָאנוּ לְפָנֶיךָ.

אָבִינוּ מַלְכֵּנוּ אֵין לָנוּ מֶלֶךְ אֶלָּא אָתָּה.

אָבִינוּ מַלְכֵּנוּ עֲשֵׂה עִמָּנוּ לְמַעַן שְׁמֶךָ.

אָבִינוּ מַלְכֵּנוּ בָּרֵךְ (בעשי״ת: חַדֵּשׁ) עָלֵינוּ שָׁנָה טוֹבָה.

אָבִינוּ מַלְכֵּנוּ בַּטֵּל מֵעָלֵינוּ כָּל גְּזֵרוֹת קָשׁוֹת.

אָבִינוּ מַלְכֵּנוּ בַּטֵּל מַחְשְׁבוֹת שׂוֹנְאֵינוּ.

אָבִינוּ מַלְכֵּנוּ הָפֵר עֲצַת אוֹיְבֵינוּ.

אָבִינוּ מַלְכֵּנוּ כַּלֵּה כָּל צַר וּמַשְׂטִין מֵעָלֵינוּ.

אָבִינוּ מַלְכֵּנוּ סְתוֹם פִּיּוֹת מַשְׂטִינֵינוּ וּמְקַטְרִיגֵינוּ.

אָבִינוּ מַלְכֵּנוּ כַּלֵּה דֶּבֶר וְחֶרֶב וְרָעָב וּשְׁבִי וּמַשְׁחִית וְעָוֹן
וּשְׁמַד מִבְּנֵי בְרִיתֶךָ.

אָבִינוּ מַלְכֵּנוּ מְנַע מַגֵּפָה מִנַּחֲלָתֶךָ.

אָבִינוּ מַלְכֵּנוּ סְלַח וּמְחַל לְכָל עֲוֹנוֹתֵינוּ.

אָבִינוּ מַלְכֵּנוּ מְחֵה וְהַעֲבֵר פְּשָׁעֵינוּ וְחַטֹּאתֵינוּ מִנֶּגֶד עֵינֶיךָ.

אָבִינוּ מַלְכֵּנוּ מְחוֹק בְּרַחֲמֶיךָ כָּל שִׁטְרֵי חוֹבוֹתֵינוּ.

אָבִינוּ מַלְכֵּנוּ הַחֲזִירֵנוּ בִּתְשׁוּבָה שְׁלֵמָה לְפָנֶיךָ.

אָבִינוּ מַלְכֵּנוּ שְׁלַח רְפוּאָה שְׁלֵמָה לְחוֹלֵי עַמֶּךָ.

אָבִינוּ מַלְכֵּנוּ קְרַע רוֹעַ גְּזַר דִּינֵנוּ.

אָבִינוּ מַלְכֵּנוּ זָכְרֵנוּ בְּזִכָּרוֹן טוֹב לְפָנֶיךָ.

On a public day of fasting:

אָבִינוּ מַלְכֵּנוּ זָכְרֵנוּ לְחַיִּים טוֹבִים.

אָבִינוּ מַלְכֵּנוּ זָכְרֵנוּ לִגְאֻלָּה וִישׁוּעָה.

אָבִינוּ מַלְכֵּנוּ זָכְרֵנוּ לְפַרְנָסָה וְכַלְכָּלָה.

אָבִינוּ מַלְכֵּנוּ זָכְרֵנוּ לִזְכֻיּוֹת.

אָבִינוּ מַלְכֵּנוּ זָכְרֵנוּ לִסְלִיחָה וּמְחִילָה.

Between Rosh Hashanah and Yom Kippur:

אָבִינוּ מַלְכֵּנוּ כָּתְבֵנוּ בְּסֵפֶר חַיִּים טוֹבִים

אָבִינוּ מַלְכֵּנוּ כָּתְבֵנוּ בְּסֵפֶר גְּאֻלָּה וִישׁוּעָה.

אָבִינוּ מַלְכֵּנוּ כָּתְבֵנוּ בְּסֵפֶר פַּרְנָסָה וְכַלְכָּלָה.

אָבִינוּ מַלְכֵּנוּ כָּתְבֵנוּ בְּסֵפֶר זְכֻיּוֹת.

אָבִינוּ מַלְכֵּנוּ כָּתְבֵנוּ בְּסֵפֶר סְלִיחָה וּמְחִילָה.

אָבִינוּ מַלְכֵּנוּ הַצְמַח לָנוּ יְשׁוּעָה בְּקָרוֹב.

אָבִינוּ מַלְכֵּנוּ הָרֵם קֶרֶן יִשְׂרָאֵל עַמֶּךָ.

אָבִינוּ מַלְכֵּנוּ הָרֵם קֶרֶן מְשִׁיחֶךָ.

אָבִינוּ מַלְכֵּנוּ מַלֵּא יָדֵינוּ מִבִּרְכוֹתֶיךָ.

אָבִינוּ מַלְכֵּנוּ מַלֵּא אֲסָמֵינוּ שָׂבָע.

אָבִינוּ מַלְכֵּנוּ שְׁמַע קוֹלֵנוּ חוּס וְרַחֵם עָלֵינוּ.

אָבִינוּ מַלְכֵּנוּ קַבֵּל בְּרַחֲמִים וּבְרָצוֹן אֶת תְּפִלָּתֵנוּ.

אָבִינוּ מַלְכֵּנוּ פְּתַח שַׁעֲרֵי שָׁמַיִם לִתְפִלָּתֵנוּ.

אָבִינוּ מַלְכֵּנוּ זְכוֹר כִּי עָפָר אֲנָחְנוּ.

אָבִינוּ מַלְכֵּנוּ נָא אַל תְּשִׁיבֵנוּ רֵיקָם מִלְּפָנֶיךָ.

אָבִינוּ מַלְכֵּנוּ תְּהֵא הַשָּׁעָה הַזֹּאת שְׁעַת רַחֲמִים וְעֵת רָצוֹן מִלְּפָנֶיךָ.

אָבִינוּ מַלְכֵּנוּ חֲמוֹל עָלֵינוּ וְעַל עוֹלְלֵנוּ וְטַפֵּנוּ.

אָבִינוּ מַלְכֵּנוּ עֲשֵׂה לְמַעַן הֲרוּגִים עַל שֵׁם קָדְשֶׁךָ.

אָבִינוּ מַלְכֵּנוּ עֲשֵׂה לְמַעַן טְבוּחִים עַל יִחוּדֶךָ.

אָבִינוּ מַלְכֵּנוּ עֲשֵׂה לְמַעַן בָּאֵי בָאֵשׁ וּבַמַּיִם עַל קִדּוּשׁ שְׁמֶךָ.

אָבִינוּ מַלְכֵּנוּ נְקוֹם נִקְמַת דַּם עֲבָדֶיךָ הַשָּׁפוּךְ.

אָבִינוּ מַלְכֵּנוּ עֲשֵׂה לְמַעַנְךָ אִם לֹא לְמַעֲנֵנוּ.

אָבִינוּ מַלְכֵּנוּ עֲשֵׂה לְמַעֲנָךְ וְהוֹשִׁיעֵנוּ.

אָבִינוּ מַלְכֵּנוּ עֲשֵׂה לְמַעַן רַחֲמֶיךָ הָרַבִּים.

אָבִינוּ מַלְכֵּנוּ עֲשֵׂה לְמַעַן שִׁמְךָ הַגָּדוֹל, הַגִּבּוֹר וְהַנּוֹרָא
שֶׁנִּקְרָא עָלֵינוּ.

אָבִינוּ מַלְכֵּנוּ חָנֵּנוּ וַעֲנֵנוּ, כִּי אֵין בָּנוּ מַעֲשִׂים, עֲשֵׂה עִמָּנוּ
צְדָקָה וָחֶסֶד וְהוֹשִׁיעֵנוּ.

וַיֹּאמֶר דָּוִד אֶל גָּד, צַר לִי מְאֹד, נִפְּלָה נָּא בְיַד יְיָ, כִּי רַבִּים
רַחֲמָיו וּבְיַד אָדָם אַל אֶפֹּלָה:

רַחוּם וְחַנּוּן חָטָאתִי לְפָנֶיךָ, יְיָ מָלֵא רַחֲמִים, רַחֵם עָלַי וְקַבֵּל
תַּחֲנוּנַי: יְיָ אַל בְּאַפְּךָ תוֹכִיחֵנִי, וְאַל בַּחֲמָתְךָ תְיַסְּרֵנִי : חָנֵּנִי
יְיָ כִּי אֻמְלַל אָנִי, רְפָאֵנִי יְיָ, כִּי נִבְהֲלוּ עֲצָמָי: וְנַפְשִׁי נִבְהֲלָה
מְאֹד, וְאַתָּה יְיָ עַד מָתָי: שׁוּבָה יְיָ חַלְּצָה נַפְשִׁי, הוֹשִׁיעֵנִי
לְמַעַן חַסְדֶּךָ: כִּי אֵין בַּמָּוֶת זִכְרֶךָ, בִּשְׁאוֹל מִי יוֹדֶה לָּךְ:
יָגַעְתִּי בְּאַנְחָתִי, אַשְׂחֶה בְכָל לַיְלָה מִטָּתִי, בְּדִמְעָתִי עַרְשִׂי
אַמְסֶה: עָשְׁשָׁה מִכַּעַס עֵינִי, עָתְקָה בְּכָל צוֹרְרָי: סוּרוּ מִמֶּנִּי
כָּל פֹּעֲלֵי אָוֶן, כִּי שָׁמַע יְיָ קוֹל בִּכְיִי: שָׁמַע יְיָ תְּחִנָּתִי, יְיָ
תְּפִלָּתִי יִקָּח: יֵבֹשׁוּ וְיִבָּהֲלוּ מְאֹד כָּל אֹיְבָי, יָשֻׁבוּ יֵבֹשׁוּ רָגַע:

שׁוֹמֵר יִשְׂרָאֵל. שְׁמוֹר שְׁאֵרִית יִשְׂרָאֵל. וְאַל יֹאבַד יִשְׂרָאֵל.
הָאוֹמְרִים שְׁמַע יִשְׂרָאֵל:

שׁוֹמֵר גּוֹי אֶחָד. שְׁמוֹר שְׁאֵרִית עַם אֶחָד. וְאַל יֹאבַד גּוֹי אֶחָד. הַמְיַחֲדִים שִׁמְךָ יְיָ אֱלֹהֵינוּ יְיָ אֶחָד:

שׁוֹמֵר גּוֹי קָדוֹשׁ. שְׁמוֹר שְׁאֵרִית עַם קָדוֹשׁ. וְאַל יֹאבַד גּוֹי קָדוֹשׁ. הַמְשַׁלְּשִׁים בְּשָׁלֹשׁ קְדֻשּׁוֹת לְקָדוֹשׁ:

מִתְרַצֶּה בְּרַחֲמִים וּמִתְפַּיֵּס בְּתַחֲנוּנִים, הִתְרַצֵּה וְהִתְפַּיֵּס לְדוֹר עָנִי כִּי אֵין עוֹזֵר: אָבִינוּ מַלְכֵּנוּ, חָנֵּנוּ וַעֲנֵנוּ כִּי אֵין בָּנוּ מַעֲשִׂים, עֲשֵׂה עִמָּנוּ צְדָקָה וָחֶסֶד וְהוֹשִׁיעֵנוּ:

וַאֲנַחְנוּ לֹא נֵדַע מַה נַּעֲשֶׂה, כִּי עָלֶיךָ עֵינֵינוּ: זְכֹר רַחֲמֶיךָ יְיָ וַחֲסָדֶיךָ, כִּי מֵעוֹלָם הֵמָּה: יְהִי חַסְדְּךָ יְיָ עָלֵינוּ, כַּאֲשֶׁר יִחַלְנוּ לָךְ: אַל תִּזְכָּר לָנוּ עֲוֹנוֹת רִאשׁוֹנִים, מַהֵר יְקַדְּמוּנוּ רַחֲמֶיךָ, כִּי דַלּוֹנוּ מְאֹד: חָנֵּנוּ יְיָ חָנֵּנוּ, כִּי רַב שָׂבַעְנוּ בוּז: בְּרֹגֶז רַחֵם תִּזְכּוֹר. כִּי הוּא יָדַע יִצְרֵנוּ, זְכוּר כִּי עָפָר אֲנָחְנוּ: עָזְרֵנוּ אֱלֹהֵי יִשְׁעֵנוּ עַל דְּבַר כְּבוֹד שְׁמֶךָ, וְהַצִּילֵנוּ וְכַפֵּר עַל חַטֹּאתֵינוּ לְמַעַן שְׁמֶךָ:

יִתְגַּדַּל וְיִתְקַדַּשׁ שְׁמֵהּ רַבָּא. בְּעָלְמָא דִּי בְרָא כִרְעוּתֵהּ, וְיַמְלִיךְ מַלְכוּתֵהּ בְּחַיֵּיכוֹן וּבְיוֹמֵיכוֹן וּבְחַיֵּי דְכָל בֵּית יִשְׂרָאֵל. בַּעֲגָלָא וּבִזְמַן קָרִיב וְאִמְרוּ אָמֵן:

יְהֵא שְׁמֵהּ רַבָּא מְבָרַךְ לְעָלַם וּלְעָלְמֵי עָלְמַיָּא:

יִתְבָּרַךְ וְיִשְׁתַּבַּח, וְיִתְפָּאַר וְיִתְרוֹמַם וְיִתְנַשֵּׂא וְיִתְהַדָּר וְיִתְעַלֶּה וְיִתְהַלָּל שְׁמֵהּ דְּקֻדְשָׁא בְּרִיךְ הוּא לְעֵלָּא מִן כָּל (בעשי"ת לְעֵלָּא וּלְעֵלָּא מִכָּל) בִּרְכָתָא וְשִׁירָתָא, תֻּשְׁבְּחָתָא וְנֶחֱמָתָא, דַּאֲמִירָן בְּעָלְמָא, וְאִמְרוּ אָמֵן:

תִּתְקַבֵּל צְלוֹתְהוֹן וּבָעוּתְהוֹן דְּכָל (בֵּית) יִשְׂרָאֵל קֳדָם אֲבוּהוֹן דִּי בִשְׁמַיָּא וְאִמְרוּ אָמֵן:

יְהֵא שְׁלָמָא רַבָּא מִן שְׁמַיָּא וְחַיִּים עָלֵינוּ וְעַל כָּל יִשְׂרָאֵל, וְאִמְרוּ אָמֵן:

עֹשֶׂה שָׁלוֹם בִּמְרוֹמָיו הוּא יַעֲשֶׂה שָׁלוֹם עָלֵינוּ וְעַל כָּל יִשְׂרָאֵל, וְאִמְרוּ אָמֵן:

עָלֵינוּ לְשַׁבֵּחַ לַאֲדוֹן הַכֹּל, לָתֵת גְּדֻלָּה לְיוֹצֵר בְּרֵאשִׁית, שֶׁלֹּא עָשָׂנוּ כְּגוֹיֵי הָאֲרָצוֹת, וְלֹא שָׂמָנוּ כְּמִשְׁפְּחוֹת הָאֲדָמָה, שֶׁלֹּא שָׂם חֶלְקֵנוּ כָּהֶם, וְגֹרָלֵנוּ כְּכָל הֲמוֹנָם (שֶׁהֵם מִשְׁתַּחֲוִים לְהֶבֶל וָרִיק וּמִתְפַּלְּלִים אֶל אֵל לֹא יוֹשִׁיעַ) וַאֲנַחְנוּ כּוֹרְעִים וּמִשְׁתַּחֲוִים וּמוֹדִים, לִפְנֵי מֶלֶךְ, מַלְכֵי הַמְּלָכִים, הַקָּדוֹשׁ בָּרוּךְ הוּא. שֶׁהוּא נוֹטֶה שָׁמַיִם וְיֹסֵד אָרֶץ, וּמוֹשַׁב יְקָרוֹ בַּשָּׁמַיִם מִמַּעַל, וּשְׁכִינַת עֻזּוֹ בְּגָבְהֵי מְרוֹמִים, הוּא אֱלֹהֵינוּ אֵין עוֹד. אֱמֶת מַלְכֵּנוּ אֶפֶס זוּלָתוֹ, כַּכָּתוּב בְּתוֹרָתוֹ: וְיָדַעְתָּ הַיּוֹם וַהֲשֵׁבֹתָ אֶל לְבָבֶךָ, כִּי יְיָ הוּא הָאֱלֹהִים בַּשָּׁמַיִם מִמַּעַל, וְעַל הָאָרֶץ מִתָּחַת, אֵין עוֹד:

עַל כֵּן נְקַוֶּה לְךָ יְיָ אֱלֹהֵינוּ, לִרְאוֹת מְהֵרָה בְּתִפְאֶרֶת עֻזֶּךָ, לְהַעֲבִיר גִּלּוּלִים מִן הָאָרֶץ וְהָאֱלִילִים כָּרוֹת יִכָּרֵתוּן . לְתַקֵּן עוֹלָם בְּמַלְכוּת שַׁדַּי, וְכָל בְּנֵי בָשָׂר יִקְרְאוּ בִשְׁמֶךָ. לְהַפְנוֹת אֵלֶיךָ כָּל רִשְׁעֵי אָרֶץ. יַכִּירוּ וְיֵדְעוּ כָּל יוֹשְׁבֵי תֵבֵל, כִּי לְךָ תִּכְרַע כָּל בֶּרֶךְ, תִּשָּׁבַע כָּל לָשׁוֹן: לְפָנֶיךָ יְיָ אֱלֹהֵינוּ יִכְרְעוּ וְיִפֹּלוּ. וְלִכְבוֹד שִׁמְךָ יְקָר יִתֵּנוּ. וִיקַבְּלוּ כֻלָּם אֶת עֹל מַלְכוּתֶךָ. וְתִמְלֹךְ עֲלֵיהֶם מְהֵרָה לְעוֹלָם וָעֶד. כִּי הַמַּלְכוּת

שֶׁלְּךָ הִיא, וּלְעוֹלְמֵי עַד תִּמְלוֹךְ בְּכָבוֹד: כַּכָּתוּב בְּתוֹרָתֶךָ, יְיָ יִמְלֹךְ לְעוֹלָם וָעֶד: וְנֶאֱמַר, וְהָיָה יְיָ לְמֶלֶךְ עַל כָּל הָאָרֶץ, בַּיּוֹם הַהוּא יִהְיֶה יְיָ אֶחָד, וּשְׁמוֹ אֶחָד:

אַל תִּירָא מִפַּחַד פִּתְאֹם, וּמִשֹּׁאַת רְשָׁעִים כִּי תָבֹא: עֻצוּ עֵצָה וְתֻפָר, דַּבְּרוּ דָבָר וְלֹא יָקוּם, כִּי עִמָּנוּ אֵל: וְעַד זִקְנָה אֲנִי הוּא, וְעַד שֵׂיבָה אֲנִי אֶסְבֹּל, אֲנִי עָשִׂיתִי וַאֲנִי אֶשָּׂא, וַאֲנִי אֶסְבֹּל וַאֲמַלֵּט:

קדיש יתום

יִתְגַּדַּל וְיִתְקַדַּשׁ שְׁמֵהּ רַבָּא. בְּעָלְמָא דִּי בְרָא כִרְעוּתֵהּ, וְיַמְלִיךְ מַלְכוּתֵהּ בְּחַיֵּיכוֹן וּבְיוֹמֵיכוֹן וּבְחַיֵּי דְכָל בֵּית יִשְׂרָאֵל. בַּעֲגָלָא וּבִזְמַן קָרִיב וְאִמְרוּ אָמֵן:

יְהֵא שְׁמֵהּ רַבָּא מְבָרַךְ לְעָלַם וּלְעָלְמֵי עָלְמַיָּא:

יִתְבָּרַךְ וְיִשְׁתַּבַּח, וְיִתְפָּאַר וְיִתְרוֹמַם וְיִתְנַשֵּׂא וְיִתְהַדָּר וְיִתְעַלֶּה וְיִתְהַלָּל שְׁמֵהּ דְּקֻדְשָׁא בְּרִיךְ הוּא לְעֵלָּא מִן כָּל (בעשי"ת לְעֵלָּא וּלְעֵלָּא מִכָּל) בִּרְכָתָא וְשִׁירָתָא, תֻּשְׁבְּחָתָא וְנֶחֱמָתָא, דַּאֲמִירָן בְּעָלְמָא, וְאִמְרוּ אָמֵן:

יְהֵא שְׁלָמָא רַבָּא מִן שְׁמַיָּא וְחַיִּים עָלֵינוּ וְעַל כָּל יִשְׂרָאֵל, וְאִמְרוּ אָמֵן:

עֹשֶׂה שָׁלוֹם בִּמְרוֹמָיו הוּא יַעֲשֶׂה שָׁלוֹם עָלֵינוּ וְעַל כָּל יִשְׂרָאֵל, וְאִמְרוּ אָמֵן:

מעריב לחול

וְהוּא רַחוּם יְכַפֵּר עָוֹן וְלֹא יַשְׁחִית, וְהִרְבָּה לְהָשִׁיב אַפּוֹ וְלֹא יָעִיר כָּל חֲמָתוֹ. יְיָ הוֹשִׁיעָה הַמֶּלֶךְ יַעֲנֵנוּ בְיוֹם קָרְאֵנוּ:

חַזָּן: בָּרְכוּ אֶת יְיָ הַמְבוֹרָךְ:

קָהָל וְחַזָּן: בָּרוּךְ יְיָ הַמְבוֹרָךְ לְעוֹלָם וָעֶד:

בָּרוּךְ אַתָּה יְיָ , אֱלֹהֵינוּ מֶלֶךְ הָעוֹלָם, אֲשֶׁר בִּדְבָרוֹ מַעֲרִיב עֲרָבִים, בְּחָכְמָה פּוֹתֵחַ שְׁעָרִים, וּבִתְבוּנָה מְשַׁנֶּה עִתִּים, וּמַחֲלִיף אֶת הַזְּמַנִּים, וּמְסַדֵּר אֶת הַכּוֹכָבִים, בְּמִשְׁמְרוֹתֵיהֶם בָּרָקִיעַ כִּרְצוֹנוֹ. בּוֹרֵא יוֹם וָלָיְלָה, גּוֹלֵל אוֹר מִפְּנֵי חֹשֶׁךְ, וְחֹשֶׁךְ מִפְּנֵי אוֹר. וּמַעֲבִיר יוֹם וּמֵבִיא לָיְלָה, וּמַבְדִּיל בֵּין יוֹם וּבֵין לָיְלָה, יְיָ צְבָאוֹת שְׁמוֹ. אֵל חַי וְקַיָּם, תָּמִיד יִמְלוֹךְ עָלֵינוּ לְעוֹלָם וָעֶד. בָּרוּךְ אַתָּה יְיָ, הַמַּעֲרִיב עֲרָבִים:

אַהֲבַת עוֹלָם בֵּית יִשְׂרָאֵל עַמְּךָ אָהַבְתָּ, תּוֹרָה וּמִצְוֹת, חֻקִּים וּמִשְׁפָּטִים, אוֹתָנוּ לִמַּדְתָּ. עַל כֵּן יְיָ אֱלֹהֵינוּ, בְּשָׁכְבֵּנוּ וּבְקוּמֵנוּ נָשִׂיחַ בְּחֻקֶּיךָ, וְנִשְׂמַח בְּדִבְרֵי תוֹרָתֶךָ וּבְמִצְוֹתֶיךָ לְעוֹלָם וָעֶד. כִּי הֵם חַיֵּינוּ וְאֹרֶךְ יָמֵינוּ, וּבָהֶם נֶהְגֶּה יוֹמָם וָלָיְלָה, וְאַהֲבָתְךָ אַל תָּסִיר מִמֶּנּוּ לְעוֹלָמִים. בָּרוּךְ אַתָּה יְיָ, אוֹהֵב עַמּוֹ יִשְׂרָאֵל:

(יָחִיד אוֹמֵר: אֵל מֶלֶךְ נָאֱמָן)

שְׁמַע יִשְׂרָאֵל, יְיָ אֱלֹהֵינוּ, יְיָ אֶחָד:

בָּרוּךְ שֵׁם כְּבוֹד מַלְכוּתוֹ לְעוֹלָם וָעֶד

וְאָהַבְתָּ אֵת יְיָ אֱלֹהֶיךָ, בְּכָל-לְבָבְךָ, וּבְכָל-נַפְשְׁךָ, וּבְכָל-מְאֹדֶךָ. וְהָיוּ הַדְּבָרִים הָאֵלֶּה, אֲשֶׁר אָנֹכִי מְצַוְּךָ הַיּוֹם, עַל-לְבָבֶךָ: וְשִׁנַּנְתָּם לְבָנֶיךָ, וְדִבַּרְתָּ בָּם בְּשִׁבְתְּךָ בְּבֵיתֶךָ, וּבְלֶכְתְּךָ בַדֶּרֶךְ, וּבְשָׁכְבְּךָ, וּבְקוּמֶךָ. וּקְשַׁרְתָּם לְאוֹת עַל-יָדֶךָ, וְהָיוּ לְטֹטָפֹת בֵּין עֵינֶיךָ, וּכְתַבְתָּם עַל מְזֻזוֹת בֵּיתֶךָ וּבִשְׁעָרֶיךָ:

וְהָיָה אִם-שָׁמֹעַ תִּשְׁמְעוּ אֶל-מִצְוֹתַי, אֲשֶׁר אָנֹכִי מְצַוֶּה אֶתְכֶם הַיּוֹם, לְאַהֲבָה אֶת יְיָ אֱלֹהֵיכֶם, וּלְעָבְדוֹ בְּכָל-לְבַבְכֶם וּבְכָל-נַפְשְׁכֶם. וְנָתַתִּי מְטַר-אַרְצְכֶם בְּעִתּוֹ, יוֹרֶה וּמַלְקוֹשׁ, וְאָסַפְתָּ דְגָנֶךָ וְתִירֹשְׁךָ וְיִצְהָרֶךָ. וְנָתַתִּי עֵשֶׂב בְּשָׂדְךָ לִבְהֶמְתֶּךָ, וְאָכַלְתָּ וְשָׂבָעְתָּ. הִשָּׁמְרוּ לָכֶם פֶּן-יִפְתֶּה לְבַבְכֶם, וְסַרְתֶּם וַעֲבַדְתֶּם אֱלֹהִים אֲחֵרִים וְהִשְׁתַּחֲוִיתֶם לָהֶם. וְחָרָה אַף-יְיָ בָּכֶם, וְעָצַר אֶת-הַשָּׁמַיִם וְלֹא-יִהְיֶה מָטָר, וְהָאֲדָמָה לֹא תִתֵּן אֶת-יְבוּלָהּ וַאֲבַדְתֶּם מְהֵרָה מֵעַל הָאָרֶץ הַטֹּבָה אֲשֶׁר יְיָ נֹתֵן לָכֶם: וְשַׂמְתֶּם אֶת דְּבָרַי אֵלֶּה עַל-לְבַבְכֶם וְעַל-נַפְשְׁכֶם וּקְשַׁרְתֶּם אֹתָם לְאוֹת עַל-יֶדְכֶם, וְהָיוּ לְטוֹטָפֹת בֵּין עֵינֵיכֶם: וְלִמַּדְתֶּם אֹתָם אֶת-בְּנֵיכֶם, לְדַבֵּר בָּם, בְּשִׁבְתְּךָ בְּבֵיתֶךָ, וּבְלֶכְתְּךָ בַדֶּרֶךְ, וּבְשָׁכְבְּךָ וּבְקוּמֶךָ: וּכְתַבְתָּם עַל-מְזוּזוֹת בֵּיתֶךָ וּבִשְׁעָרֶיךָ: לְמַעַן יִרְבּוּ יְמֵיכֶם וִימֵי בְנֵיכֶם עַל הָאֲדָמָה אֲשֶׁר נִשְׁבַּע יְיָ לַאֲבֹתֵיכֶם לָתֵת לָהֶם, כִּימֵי הַשָּׁמַיִם עַל-הָאָרֶץ:

וַיֹּאמֶר יְיָ אֶל־מֹשֶׁה לֵּאמֹר: דַּבֵּר אֶל־בְּנֵי יִשְׂרָאֵל וְאָמַרְתָּ
אֲלֵהֶם: וְעָשׂוּ לָהֶם צִיצִת עַל־כַּנְפֵי בִגְדֵיהֶם לְדֹרֹתָם, וְנָתְנוּ
עַל־צִיצִת הַכָּנָף פְּתִיל תְּכֵלֶת. וְהָיָה לָכֶם לְצִיצִת, וּרְאִיתֶם
אֹתוֹ וּזְכַרְתֶּם אֶת־כָּל־מִצְוֹת יְיָ, וַעֲשִׂיתֶם אֹתָם, וְלֹא תָתוּרוּ
אַחֲרֵי לְבַבְכֶם וְאַחֲרֵי עֵינֵיכֶם, אֲשֶׁר־אַתֶּם זֹנִים אַחֲרֵיהֶם:
לְמַעַן תִּזְכְּרוּ וַעֲשִׂיתֶם אֶת־כָּל־מִצְוֹתָי, וִהְיִיתֶם קְדֹשִׁים
לֵאלֹהֵיכֶם: אֲנִי יְיָ אֱלֹהֵיכֶם, אֲשֶׁר הוֹצֵאתִי אֶתְכֶם מֵאֶרֶץ
מִצְרַיִם, לִהְיוֹת לָכֶם לֵאלֹהִים, אֲנִי יְיָ אֱלֹהֵיכֶם:

אֱמֶת

וֶאֱמוּנָה כָּל זֹאת, וְקַיָּם עָלֵינוּ, כִּי הוּא יְיָ אֱלֹהֵינוּ וְאֵין
זוּלָתוֹ, וַאֲנַחְנוּ יִשְׂרָאֵל עַמּוֹ. הַפּוֹדֵנוּ מִיַּד מְלָכִים, מַלְכֵּנוּ
הַגּוֹאֲלֵנוּ מִכַּף כָּל־הֶעָרִיצִים. הָאֵל הַנִּפְרָע לָנוּ מִצָּרֵינוּ,
וְהַמְשַׁלֵּם גְּמוּל לְכָל אֹיְבֵי נַפְשֵׁנוּ, הָעֹשֶׂה גְדוֹלוֹת עַד אֵין
חֵקֶר, וְנִפְלָאוֹת עַד אֵין מִסְפָּר. הַשָּׂם נַפְשֵׁנוּ בַּחַיִּים, וְלֹא נָתַן
לַמּוֹט רַגְלֵנוּ, הַמַּדְרִיכֵנוּ עַל בָּמוֹת אוֹיְבֵינוּ, וַיָּרֶם קַרְנֵנוּ,
עַל כָּל שׂוֹנְאֵינוּ, הָעֹשֶׂה לָּנוּ נִסִּים וּנְקָמָה בְּפַרְעֹה, אוֹתוֹת
וּמוֹפְתִים בְּאַדְמַת בְּנֵי חָם. הַמַּכֶּה בְּעֶבְרָתוֹ כָּל בְּכוֹרֵי
מִצְרַיִם, וַיּוֹצֵא אֶת עַמּוֹ יִשְׂרָאֵל מִתּוֹכָם, לְחֵרוּת עוֹלָם.
הַמַּעֲבִיר בָּנָיו בֵּין גִּזְרֵי יַם סוּף, אֶת רוֹדְפֵיהֶם וְאֶת
שׂוֹנְאֵיהֶם, בִּתְהוֹמוֹת טִבַּע, וְרָאוּ בָנָיו גְּבוּרָתוֹ. שִׁבְּחוּ וְהוֹדוּ
לִשְׁמוֹ. וּמַלְכוּתוֹ בְּרָצוֹן קִבְּלוּ עֲלֵיהֶם, מֹשֶׁה וּבְנֵי יִשְׂרָאֵל לְךָ
עָנוּ שִׁירָה בְּשִׂמְחָה רַבָּה, וְאָמְרוּ כֻלָּם:

מִי כָמֹכָה בָּאֵלִים יְיָ, מִי כָּמֹכָה נֶאְדָּר בַּקֹּדֶשׁ, נוֹרָא
תְהִלֹּת, עֹשֵׂה פֶלֶא: מַלְכוּתְךָ רָאוּ בָנֶיךָ, בּוֹקֵעַ יָם לִפְנֵי

מֹשֶׁה, זֶה אֵלִי עָנוּ וְאָמְרוּ: יְיָ יִמְלוֹךְ לְעוֹלָם וָעֶד. וְנֶאֱמַר: כִּי פָדָה יְיָ אֶת יַעֲקֹב, וּגְאָלוֹ מִיַּד חָזָק מִמֶּנּוּ. בָּרוּךְ אַתָּה יְיָ גָּאַל יִשְׂרָאֵל:

הַשְׁכִּיבֵנוּ יְיָ אֱלֹהֵינוּ לְשָׁלוֹם, וְהַעֲמִידֵנוּ מַלְכֵּנוּ לְחַיִּים וּפְרוֹשׂ עָלֵינוּ סֻכַּת שְׁלוֹמֶךָ וְתַקְּנֵנוּ בְּעֵצָה טוֹבָה מִלְּפָנֶיךָ, וְהוֹשִׁיעֵנוּ לְמַעַן שְׁמֶךָ, וְהָגֵן בַּעֲדֵנוּ, וְהָסֵר מֵעָלֵינוּ אוֹיֵב, דֶּבֶר, וְחֶרֶב, וְרָעָב וְיָגוֹן, וְהָסֵר שָׂטָן מִלְּפָנֵינוּ וּמֵאַחֲרֵינוּ, וּבְצֵל כְּנָפֶיךָ תַּסְתִּירֵנוּ. כִּי אֵל שׁוֹמְרֵנוּ וּמַצִּילֵנוּ אַתָּה, כִּי אֵל מֶלֶךְ חַנּוּן וְרַחוּם אָתָּה, וּשְׁמוֹר צֵאתֵנוּ וּבוֹאֵנוּ, לְחַיִּים וּלְשָׁלוֹם, מֵעַתָּה וְעַד עוֹלָם. בָּרוּךְ אַתָּה יְיָ, שׁוֹמֵר עַמּוֹ יִשְׂרָאֵל לָעַד:

The following is not said in Eretz Yisrael

(בָּרוּךְ יְיָ לְעוֹלָם, אָמֵן וְאָמֵן. בָּרוּךְ יְיָ מִצִּיּוֹן שֹׁכֵן יְרוּשָׁלָיִם הַלְלוּיָהּ. בָּרוּךְ יְיָ אֱלֹהִים אֱלֹהֵי יִשְׂרָאֵל, עֹשֵׂה נִפְלָאוֹת לְבַדּוֹ. וּבָרוּךְ שֵׁם כְּבוֹדוֹ לְעוֹלָם, וְיִמָּלֵא כְבוֹדוֹ אֶת כָּל הָאָרֶץ, אָמֵן וְאָמֵן. יְהִי כְבוֹד יְיָ לְעוֹלָם, יִשְׂמַח יְיָ בְּמַעֲשָׂיו. יְהִי שֵׁם יְיָ מְבוֹרָךְ, מֵעַתָּה וְעַד עוֹלָם, כִּי לֹא יִטֹּשׁ יְיָ אֶת עַמּוֹ בַּעֲבוּר שְׁמוֹ הַגָּדוֹל, כִּי

הוֹאִיל יְיָ לַעֲשׂוֹת אֶתְכֶם לוֹ לְעָם. וַיַּרְא כָּל הָעָם וַיִּפְּלוּ עַל פְּנֵיהֶם, וַיֹּאמְרוּ: יְיָ הוּא הָאֱלֹהִים, יְיָ הוּא הָאֱלֹהִים. וְהָיָה יְיָ לְמֶלֶךְ עַל כָּל הָאָרֶץ, בַּיּוֹם הַהוּא יִהְיֶה יְיָ אֶחָד וּשְׁמוֹ אֶחָד. יְהִי חַסְדְּךָ יְיָ עָלֵינוּ, כַּאֲשֶׁר יִחַלְנוּ לָךְ. הוֹשִׁיעֵנוּ יְיָ אֱלֹהֵינוּ, וְקַבְּצֵנוּ מִן הַגּוֹיִם, לְהוֹדוֹת לְשֵׁם קָדְשֶׁךָ, לְהִשְׁתַּבֵּחַ בִּתְהִלָּתֶךָ. כָּל גּוֹיִם אֲשֶׁר עָשִׂיתָ יָבוֹאוּ וְיִשְׁתַּחֲווּ לְפָנֶיךָ אֲדֹנָי, וִיכַבְּדוּ לִשְׁמֶךָ. כִּי גָדוֹל אַתָּה וְעֹשֵׂה נִפְלָאוֹת אַתָּה אֱלֹהִים

לְבַדֶּךָ. וַאֲנַחְנוּ עַמְּךָ וְצֹאן מַרְעִיתֶךָ, נוֹדֶה לְךָ לְעוֹלָם, לְדוֹר
וָדוֹר נְסַפֵּר תְּהִלָּתֶךָ. בָּרוּךְ יְיָ בַּיּוֹם, בָּרוּךְ יְיָ בַּלַּיְלָה, בָּרוּךְ
יְיָ בְּשָׁכְבֵנוּ, בָּרוּךְ יְיָ בְּקוּמֵנוּ. כִּי בְיָדְךָ נַפְשׁוֹת הַחַיִּים
וְהַמֵּתִים, אֲשֶׁר בְּיָדוֹ נֶפֶשׁ כָּל חָי וְרוּחַ כָּל בְּשַׂר אִישׁ. בְּיָדְךָ
אַפְקִיד רוּחִי, פָּדִיתָה אוֹתִי יְיָ אֵל אֱמֶת. אֱלֹהֵינוּ שֶׁבַּשָּׁמַיִם,
יַחֵד שִׁמְךָ, וְקַיֵּם מַלְכוּתְךָ תָּמִיד, וּמְלוֹךְ עָלֵינוּ לְעוֹלָם וָעֶד:

יִרְאוּ עֵינֵינוּ, וְיִשְׂמַח לִבֵּנוּ, וְתָגֵל נַפְשֵׁנוּ, בִּישׁוּעָתְךָ בֶּאֱמֶת,
בֶּאֱמֹר לְצִיּוֹן מָלַךְ אֱלֹהָיִךְ. יְיָ מֶלֶךְ, יְיָ מָלָךְ, יְיָ יִמְלוֹךְ
לְעוֹלָם וָעֶד, כִּי הַמַּלְכוּת שֶׁלְּךָ הִיא, וּלְעוֹלְמֵי עַד תִּמְלוֹךְ
בְּכָבוֹד, כִּי אֵין לָנוּ מֶלֶךְ אֶלָּא אָתָּה. בָּרוּךְ אַתָּה יְיָ, הַמֶּלֶךְ
בִּכְבוֹדוֹ, תָּמִיד יִמְלוֹךְ עָלֵינוּ לְעוֹלָם וָעֶד, וְעַל כָּל מַעֲשָׂיו:)

יִתְגַּדַּל וְיִתְקַדַּשׁ שְׁמֵהּ רַבָּא. בְּעָלְמָא דִּי בְרָא כִרְעוּתֵהּ, וְיַמְלִיךְ
מַלְכוּתֵהּ בְּחַיֵּיכוֹן וּבְיוֹמֵיכוֹן וּבְחַיֵּי דְכָל בֵּית יִשְׂרָאֵל. בַּעֲגָלָא
וּבִזְמַן קָרִיב וְאִמְרוּ אָמֵן:

יְהֵא שְׁמֵהּ רַבָּא מְבָרַךְ לְעָלַם וּלְעָלְמֵי עָלְמַיָּא:

יִתְבָּרַךְ וְיִשְׁתַּבַּח, וְיִתְפָּאַר וְיִתְרוֹמַם וְיִתְנַשֵּׂא וְיִתְהַדָּר וְיִתְעַלֶּה
וְיִתְהַלָּל שְׁמֵהּ דְּקֻדְשָׁא בְּרִיךְ הוּא לְעֵלָּא מִן כָּל (בעשי"ת לְעֵלָּא לְעֵלָּא
וּלְעֵלָּא מִכָּל) בִּרְכָתָא וְשִׁירָתָא, תֻּשְׁבְּחָתָא וְנֶחֱמָתָא, דַּאֲמִירָן
בְּעָלְמָא, וְאִמְרוּ אָמֵן:

Shemoneh Esrei (page 33)

יִתְגַּדַּל וְיִתְקַדַּשׁ שְׁמֵהּ רַבָּא. בְּעָלְמָא דִּי בְרָא כִרְעוּתֵהּ, וְיַמְלִיךְ מַלְכוּתֵהּ בְּחַיֵּיכוֹן וּבְיוֹמֵיכוֹן וּבְחַיֵּי דְכָל בֵּית יִשְׂרָאֵל. בַּעֲגָלָא וּבִזְמַן קָרִיב וְאִמְרוּ אָמֵן:

יְהֵא שְׁמֵהּ רַבָּא מְבָרַךְ לְעָלַם וּלְעָלְמֵי עָלְמַיָּא:

יִתְבָּרַךְ וְיִשְׁתַּבַּח, וְיִתְפָּאַר וְיִתְרוֹמַם וְיִתְנַשֵּׂא וְיִתְהַדָּר וְיִתְעַלֶּה וְיִתְהַלָּל שְׁמֵהּ דְּקֻדְשָׁא בְּרִיךְ הוּא לְעֵלָּא מִן כָּל (בעשי״ת לְעֵלָּא וּלְעֵלָּא מִכָּל) בִּרְכָתָא וְשִׁירָתָא, תֻּשְׁבְּחָתָא וְנֶחֱמָתָא, דַּאֲמִירָן בְּעָלְמָא, וְאִמְרוּ אָמֵן:

תִּתְקַבַּל צְלוֹתְהוֹן וּבָעוּתְהוֹן דְּכָל (בֵּית) יִשְׂרָאֵל קֳדָם אֲבוּהוֹן דִּי בִשְׁמַיָּא וְאִמְרוּ אָמֵן:

יְהֵא שְׁלָמָא רַבָּא מִן שְׁמַיָּא וְחַיִּים עָלֵינוּ וְעַל כָּל יִשְׂרָאֵל, וְאִמְרוּ אָמֵן:

עֹשֶׂה שָׁלוֹם בִּמְרוֹמָיו הוּא יַעֲשֶׂה שָׁלוֹם עָלֵינוּ וְעַל כָּל יִשְׂרָאֵל, וְאִמְרוּ אָמֵן:

עָלֵינוּ לְשַׁבֵּחַ לַאֲדוֹן הַכֹּל, לָתֵת גְּדֻלָּה לְיוֹצֵר בְּרֵאשִׁית, שֶׁלֹּא עָשָׂנוּ כְּגוֹיֵי הָאֲרָצוֹת, וְלֹא שָׂמָנוּ כְּמִשְׁפְּחוֹת הָאֲדָמָה, שֶׁלֹּא שָׂם חֶלְקֵנוּ כָּהֶם, וְגֹרָלֵנוּ כְּכָל הֲמוֹנָם (שֶׁהֵם מִשְׁתַּחֲוִים לְהֶבֶל וָרִיק וּמִתְפַּלְלִים אֶל אֵל לֹא יוֹשִׁיעַ) וַאֲנַחְנוּ כּוֹרְעִים וּמִשְׁתַּחֲוִים וּמוֹדִים, לִפְנֵי מֶלֶךְ, מַלְכֵי הַמְּלָכִים, הַקָּדוֹשׁ בָּרוּךְ הוּא. שֶׁהוּא נוֹטֶה שָׁמַיִם וְיֹסֵד אָרֶץ, וּמוֹשַׁב יְקָרוֹ בַּשָּׁמַיִם מִמַּעַל, וּשְׁכִינַת עֻזּוֹ בְּגָבְהֵי מְרוֹמִים, הוּא אֱלֹהֵינוּ אֵין עוֹד. אֱמֶת מַלְכֵּנוּ אֶפֶס זוּלָתוֹ, כַּכָּתוּב בְּתוֹרָתוֹ: וְיָדַעְתָּ הַיּוֹם וַהֲשֵׁבֹתָ אֶל לְבָבֶךָ, כִּי יְיָ הוּא הָאֱלֹהִים בַּשָּׁמַיִם מִמַּעַל, וְעַל הָאָרֶץ מִתָּחַת, אֵין עוֹד:

עַל כֵּן נְקַוֶּה לְּךָ יְיָ אֱלֹהֵינוּ, לִרְאוֹת מְהֵרָה בְּתִפְאֶרֶת עֻזֶּךָ,
לְהַעֲבִיר גִּלּוּלִים מִן הָאָרֶץ וְהָאֱלִילִים כָּרוֹת יִכָּרֵתוּן · לְתַקֵּן
עוֹלָם בְּמַלְכוּת שַׁדַּי, וְכָל בְּנֵי בָשָׂר יִקְרְאוּ בִשְׁמֶךָ. לְהַפְנוֹת
אֵלֶיךָ כָּל רִשְׁעֵי אָרֶץ. יַכִּירוּ וְיֵדְעוּ כָּל יוֹשְׁבֵי תֵבֵל, כִּי לְךָ
תִּכְרַע כָּל בֶּרֶךְ, תִּשָּׁבַע כָּל לָשׁוֹן: לְפָנֶיךָ יְיָ אֱלֹהֵינוּ יִכְרְעוּ
וְיִפֹּלוּ. וְלִכְבוֹד שִׁמְךָ יְקָר יִתֵּנוּ. וִיקַבְּלוּ כֻלָּם אֶת עֹל
מַלְכוּתֶךָ. וְתִמְלֹךְ עֲלֵיהֶם מְהֵרָה לְעוֹלָם וָעֶד. כִּי הַמַּלְכוּת
שֶׁלְּךָ הִיא, וּלְעוֹלְמֵי עַד תִּמְלוֹךְ בְּכָבוֹד: כַּכָּתוּב בְּתוֹרָתֶךָ,
יְיָ יִמְלֹךְ לְעוֹלָם וָעֶד: וְנֶאֱמַר, וְהָיָה יְיָ לְמֶלֶךְ עַל כָּל הָאָרֶץ,
בַּיּוֹם הַהוּא יִהְיֶה יְיָ אֶחָד, וּשְׁמוֹ אֶחָד:

אַל תִּירָא מִפַּחַד פִּתְאֹם, וּמִשֹּׁאַת רְשָׁעִים כִּי תָבֹא: עֻצוּ עֵצָה
וְתֻפָר, דַּבְּרוּ דָבָר וְלֹא יָקוּם, כִּי עִמָּנוּ אֵל: וְעַד זִקְנָה אֲנִי
הוּא, וְעַד שֵׂיבָה אֲנִי אֶסְבֹּל, אֲנִי עָשִׂיתִי וַאֲנִי אֶשָּׂא, וַאֲנִי
אֶסְבֹּל וַאֲמַלֵּט:

קדיש יתום

יִתְגַּדַּל וְיִתְקַדַּשׁ שְׁמֵהּ רַבָּא. בְּעָלְמָא דִּי בְרָא כִרְעוּתֵהּ, וְיַמְלִיךְ
מַלְכוּתֵהּ בְּחַיֵּיכוֹן וּבְיוֹמֵיכוֹן וּבְחַיֵּי דְכָל בֵּית יִשְׂרָאֵל. בַּעֲגָלָא
וּבִזְמַן קָרִיב וְאִמְרוּ אָמֵן:

יְהֵא שְׁמֵהּ רַבָּא מְבָרַךְ לְעָלַם וּלְעָלְמֵי עָלְמַיָּא:

יִתְבָּרַךְ וְיִשְׁתַּבַּח, וְיִתְפָּאַר וְיִתְרוֹמַם וְיִתְנַשֵּׂא וְיִתְהַדָּר וְיִתְעַלֶּה
וְיִתְהַלָּל שְׁמֵהּ דְּקֻדְשָׁא בְּרִיךְ הוּא לְעֵלָּא מִן כָּל (בעשי״ת לְעֵלָּא
וּלְעֵלָּא מִכָּל) בִּרְכָתָא וְשִׁירָתָא, תֻּשְׁבְּחָתָא וְנֶחֱמָתָא, דַּאֲמִירָן
בְּעָלְמָא, וְאִמְרוּ אָמֵן:

יְהֵא שְׁלָמָא רַבָּא מִן שְׁמַיָּא וְחַיִּים עָלֵינוּ וְעַל כָּל יִשְׂרָאֵל, וְאִמְרוּ
אָמֵן:

עֹשֶׂה שָׁלוֹם בִּמְרוֹמָיו הוּא יַעֲשֶׂה שָׁלוֹם עָלֵינוּ וְעַל כָּל יִשְׂרָאֵל,
וְאִמְרוּ אָמֵן:

**The following is added everyday from the first day of Elul
to Shemini Atzeres during Maariv**

לְדָוִד יְיָ אוֹרִי וְיִשְׁעִי מִמִּי אִירָא, יְיָ מָעוֹז חַיַּי מִמִּי אֶפְחָד:
בִּקְרֹב עָלַי מְרֵעִים, לֶאֱכֹל אֶת בְּשָׂרִי צָרַי וְאֹיְבַי לִי הֵמָּה
כָּשְׁלוּ וְנָפָלוּ: אִם תַּחֲנֶה עָלַי מַחֲנֶה לֹא יִירָא לִבִּי, אִם תָּקוּם
עָלַי מִלְחָמָה בְּזֹאת אֲנִי בוֹטֵחַ: אַחַת שָׁאַלְתִּי מֵאֵת יְיָ, אוֹתָהּ
אֲבַקֵּשׁ שִׁבְתִּי בְּבֵית יְיָ, כָּל יְמֵי חַיַּי לַחֲזוֹת בְּנֹעַם יְיָ וּלְבַקֵּר
בְּהֵיכָלוֹ: כִּי יִצְפְּנֵנִי בְּסֻכֹּה בְּיוֹם רָעָה, יַסְתִּרֵנִי בְּסֵתֶר אָהֳלוֹ
בְּצוּר יְרוֹמְמֵנִי: וְעַתָּה יָרוּם רֹאשִׁי, עַל אֹיְבַי סְבִיבוֹתַי
וְאֶזְבְּחָה בְאָהֳלוֹ זִבְחֵי תְרוּעָה, אָשִׁירָה וַאֲזַמְּרָה לַייָ: שְׁמַע יְיָ
קוֹלִי אֶקְרָא, וְחָנֵּנִי וַעֲנֵנִי: לְךָ אָמַר לִבִּי, בַּקְּשׁוּ פָנָי, אֶת
פָּנֶיךָ יְיָ אֲבַקֵּשׁ: אַל תַּסְתֵּר פָּנֶיךָ מִמֶּנִּי, אַל תַּט בְּאַף עַבְדֶּךָ,
עֶזְרָתִי הָיִיתָ, אַל תִּטְּשֵׁנִי וְאַל תַּעַזְבֵנִי אֱלֹהֵי יִשְׁעִי: כִּי אָבִי
וְאִמִּי עֲזָבוּנִי, וַייָ יַאַסְפֵנִי: הוֹרֵנִי יְיָ דַּרְכֶּךָ, וּנְחֵנִי בְּאֹרַח
מִישׁוֹר, לְמַעַן שׁוֹרְרָי: אַל תִּתְּנֵנִי בְּנֶפֶשׁ צָרָי, כִּי קָמוּ בִי עֵדֵי
שֶׁקֶר וִיפֵחַ חָמָס: לוּלֵא הֶאֱמַנְתִּי, לִרְאוֹת בְּטוּב יְיָ בְּאֶרֶץ
חַיִּים: קַוֵּה אֶל יְיָ, חֲזַק וְיַאֲמֵץ לִבֶּךָ וְקַוֵּה אֶל יְיָ:

The following paragraph is added when praying in the house of a mourner on a day when תַּחֲנוּן is said. On a day when תַּחֲנוּן is not said, the second paragraph is said.

לַמְנַצֵּחַ לִבְנֵי קֹרַח מִזְמוֹר. שִׁמְעוּ זֹאת כָּל הָעַמִּים, הַאֲזִינוּ כָּל יֹשְׁבֵי חָלֶד. גַּם בְּנֵי אָדָם, גַּם בְּנֵי אִישׁ, יַחַד עָשִׁיר וְאֶבְיוֹן. פִּי יְדַבֵּר חָכְמוֹת, וְהָגוּת לִבִּי תְבוּנוֹת. אַטֶּה לְמָשָׁל אָזְנִי, אֶפְתַּח בְּכִנּוֹר חִידָתִי. לָמָּה אִירָא בִּימֵי רָע, עֲוֹן עֲקֵבַי יְסֻבֵּנִי. הַבֹּטְחִים עַל חֵילָם, וּבְרֹב עָשְׁרָם יִתְהַלָּלוּ. אָח לֹא פָדֹה יִפְדֶּה אִישׁ, לֹא יִתֵּן לֵאלֹהִים כָּפְרוֹ. וְיֵקַר פִּדְיוֹן נַפְשָׁם, וְחָדַל לְעוֹלָם. וִיחִי עוֹד לָנֶצַח, לֹא יִרְאֶה הַשָּׁחַת. כִּי יִרְאֶה חֲכָמִים יָמוּתוּ, יַחַד כְּסִיל וָבַעַר יֹאבֵדוּ, וְעָזְבוּ לַאֲחֵרִים חֵילָם. קִרְבָּם בָּתֵּימוֹ לְעוֹלָם, מִשְׁכְּנֹתָם לְדוֹר וָדֹר, קָרְאוּ בִשְׁמוֹתָם עֲלֵי אֲדָמוֹת. וְאָדָם בִּיקָר בַּל יָלִין, נִמְשַׁל כַּבְּהֵמוֹת נִדְמוּ. זֶה דַרְכָּם, כֵּסֶל לָמוֹ, וְאַחֲרֵיהֶם בְּפִיהֶם יִרְצוּ, סֶלָה. כַּצֹּאן לִשְׁאוֹל שַׁתּוּ, מָוֶת יִרְעֵם, וַיִּרְדּוּ בָם יְשָׁרִים לַבֹּקֶר, וְצוּרָם לְבַלּוֹת שְׁאוֹל מִזְּבֻל לוֹ. אַךְ אֱלֹהִים יִפְדֶּה נַפְשִׁי מִיַּד שְׁאוֹל, כִּי יִקָּחֵנִי סֶלָה. אַל תִּירָא כִּי יַעֲשִׁר אִישׁ, כִּי יִרְבֶּה כְּבוֹד בֵּיתוֹ. כִּי לֹא בְמוֹתוֹ יִקַּח הַכֹּל, לֹא יֵרֵד אַחֲרָיו כְּבוֹדוֹ. כִּי נַפְשׁוֹ בְּחַיָּיו יְבָרֵךְ, וְיוֹדֻךָ כִּי תֵיטִיב לָךְ. תָּבוֹא עַד דּוֹר אֲבוֹתָיו, עַד נֵצַח לֹא יִרְאוּ אוֹר. אָדָם בִּיקָר וְלֹא יָבִין, נִמְשַׁל כַּבְּהֵמוֹת נִדְמוּ.

מִכְתָּם לְדָוִד שָׁמְרֵנִי אֵל כִּי־חָסִיתִי בָךְ: אָמַרְתְּ לַיהוָה אֲדֹנָי אָתָּה טוֹבָתִי בַּל־עָלֶיךָ: לִקְדוֹשִׁים אֲשֶׁר־בָּאָרֶץ הֵמָּה וְאַדִּירֵי כָּל־חֶפְצִי־בָם: יִרְבּוּ עַצְּבוֹתָם אַחֵר מָהָרוּ בַּל־אַסִּיךְ נִסְכֵּיהֶם

מִדָּם וּבַל־אֶשָּׂא אֶת־שְׁמוֹתָם עַל־שְׂפָתָי: יְהוָֹה מְנָת־חֶלְקִי
וְכוֹסִי אַתָּה תּוֹמִיךְ גּוֹרָלִי: חֲבָלִים נָפְלוּ־לִי בַּנְּעִמִים אַף־
נַחֲלָת שָׁפְרָה עָלָי: אֲבָרֵךְ אֶת־יְהוָֹה אֲשֶׁר יְעָצָנִי אַף־לֵילוֹת
יִסְּרוּנִי כִלְיוֹתָי: שִׁוִּיתִי יְהוָֹה לְנֶגְדִּי תָמִיד כִּי מִימִינִי בַּל־
אֶמּוֹט: לָכֵן שָׂמַח לִבִּי וַיָּגֶל כְּבוֹדִי אַף־בְּשָׂרִי יִשְׁכֹּן לָבֶטַח:
כִּי לֹא־תַעֲזֹב נַפְשִׁי לִשְׁאוֹל לֹא־תִתֵּן חֲסִידְךָ לִרְאוֹת שָׁחַת:
תּוֹדִיעֵנִי אֹרַח חַיִּים שֹׂבַע שְׂמָחוֹת אֶת־פָּנֶיךָ נְעִמוֹת בִּימִינְךָ
נֶצַח:

ספירת העומר

הִנְנִי מוּכָן וּמְזֻמָּן לְקַיֵּם מִצְוַת עֲשֵׂה שֶׁל סְפִירַת הָעֹמֶר כְּמוֹ
שֶׁכָּתוּב בַּתּוֹרָה: וּסְפַרְתֶּם לָכֶם מִמָּחֳרַת הַשַּׁבָּת מִיּוֹם
הֲבִיאֲכֶם אֶת עֹמֶר הַתְּנוּפָה שֶׁבַע שַׁבָּתוֹת תְּמִימֹת תִּהְיֶינָה:
עַד מִמָּחֳרַת הַשַּׁבָּת הַשְּׁבִיעִת תִּסְפְּרוּ חֲמִשִּׁים יוֹם וְהִקְרַבְתֶּם
מִנְחָה חֲדָשָׁה לַיְיָ: וִיהִי נֹעַם יְיָ אֱלֹהֵינוּ עָלֵינוּ וּמַעֲשֵׂה יָדֵינוּ
כּוֹנְנָה עָלֵינוּ וּמַעֲשֵׂה יָדֵינוּ כּוֹנְנֵהוּ:

בָּרוּךְ אַתָּה יְיָ אֱלֹהֵינוּ מֶלֶךְ הָעוֹלָם, אֲשֶׁר קִדְּשָׁנוּ בְּמִצְוֹתָיו
וְצִוָּנוּ עַל סְפִירַת הָעֹמֶר.

טז בניסן, א' של חול המועד
הַיּוֹם יוֹם אֶחָד לָעֹמֶר. חסד שבחסד

יז בניסן, ב' של חול המועד
הַיּוֹם שְׁנֵי יָמִים לָעֹמֶר. גבורה שבחסד

יח בניסן,ג' של חול המועד

הַיּוֹם שְׁלֹשָׁה יָמִים לָעֹמֶר. תפארת שבחסד

יט בניסן, ד' של חול המועד

הַיּוֹם אַרְבָּעָה יָמִים לָעֹמֶר. נצח שבחסד

כ בניסן, ה' של חול המועד

הַיּוֹם חֲמִשָּׁה יָמִים לָעֹמֶר. הוד שבחסד

כא בניסן, שביעי של פסח

הַיּוֹם שִׁשָּׁה יָמִים לָעֹמֶר. יסוד שבחסד

כב בניסן, מוצאי יום טוב

הַיּוֹם שִׁבְעָה יָמִים שֶׁהֵם שָׁבוּעַ אֶחָד לָעֹמֶר. מלכות שבחסד

כג בניסן

הַיּוֹם שְׁמוֹנָה יָמִים שֶׁהֵם שָׁבוּעַ אֶחָד וְיוֹם אֶחָד לָעֹמֶר.
חסד שבגבורה

כד בניסן

הַיּוֹם תִּשְׁעָה יָמִים שֶׁהֵם שָׁבוּעַ אֶחָד וּשְׁנֵי יָמִים לָעֹמֶר.
גבורה שבגבורה

כה בניסן

הַיּוֹם עֲשָׂרָה יָמִים שֶׁהֵם שָׁבוּעַ אֶחָד וּשְׁלֹשָׁה יָמִים לָעֹמֶר.
תפארת שבגבורה

כו בניסן

הַיּוֹם אַחַד עָשָׂר יוֹם שֶׁהֵם שָׁבוּעַ אֶחָד וְאַרְבָּעָה יָמִים לָעֹמֶר.
נצח שבגבורה

כז בניסן

הַיּוֹם שְׁנֵים עָשָׂר יוֹם שֶׁהֵם שָׁבוּעַ אֶחָד וַחֲמִשָּׁה יָמִים לָעֹמֶר.
הוד שבגבורה

כח בניסן

הַיּוֹם שְׁלֹשָׁה עָשָׂר יוֹם שֶׁהֵם שָׁבוּעַ אֶחָד וְשִׁשָּׁה יָמִים לָעֹמֶר.
יסוד שבגבורה

כט בניסן

הַיּוֹם אַרְבָּעָה עָשָׂר יוֹם שֶׁהֵם שְׁנֵי שָׁבוּעוֹת לָעֹמֶר.
מלכות שבגבורה

ל' בניסן, א' דראש חדש

הַיּוֹם חֲמִשָּׁה עָשָׂר יוֹם שֶׁהֵם שְׁנֵי שָׁבוּעוֹת וְיוֹם אֶחָד לָעֹמֶר.
חסד שבתפארת

א' באייר, ב' דראש חדש

הַיּוֹם שִׁשָּׁה עָשָׂר יוֹם שֶׁהֵם שְׁנֵי שָׁבוּעוֹת וּשְׁנֵי יָמִים לָעֹמֶר.
גבורה שבתפארת

ב' באייר

הַיּוֹם שִׁבְעָה עָשָׂר יוֹם שֶׁהֵם שְׁנֵי שָׁבוּעוֹת וּשְׁלֹשָׁה יָמִים לָעֹמֶר. תפארת שבתפארת

ג׳ באייר

הַיּוֹם שְׁמוֹנָה עָשָׂר יוֹם שֶׁהֵם שְׁנֵי שָׁבוּעוֹת וְאַרְבָּעָה יָמִים לָעֹמֶר. נצח שבתפארת

ד׳ באייר

הַיּוֹם תִּשְׁעָה עָשָׂר יוֹם שֶׁהֵם שְׁנֵי שָׁבוּעוֹת וַחֲמִשָּׁה יָמִים לָעֹמֶר. הוד שבתפארת

ה׳ באייר, יום העצמאות

הַיּוֹם עֶשְׂרִים יוֹם שֶׁהֵם שְׁנֵי שָׁבוּעוֹת וְשִׁשָּׁה יָמִים לָעֹמֶר. יסוד שבתפארת

ו׳ באייר

הַיּוֹם אֶחָד וְעֶשְׂרִים יוֹם שֶׁהֵם שְׁלֹשָׁה שָׁבוּעוֹת לָעֹמֶר. מלכות שבתפארת

ז׳ באייר

הַיּוֹם שְׁנַיִם וְעֶשְׂרִים יוֹם שֶׁהֵם שְׁלֹשָׁה שָׁבוּעוֹת וְיוֹם אֶחָד לָעֹמֶר. חסד שבנצח

ח׳ באייר

הַיּוֹם שְׁלֹשָׁה וְעֶשְׂרִים יוֹם שֶׁהֵם שְׁלֹשָׁה שָׁבוּעוֹת וּשְׁנֵי יָמִים לָעֹמֶר. גבורה שבנצח

ט׳ באייר

הַיּוֹם אַרְבָּעָה וְעֶשְׂרִים יוֹם שֶׁהֵם שְׁלֹשָׁה שָׁבוּעוֹת וּשְׁלֹשָׁה יָמִים לָעֹמֶר. תפארת שבנצח

י׳ באייר

הַיּוֹם חֲמִשָּׁה וְעֶשְׂרִים יוֹם שֶׁהֵם שְׁלֹשָׁה שָׁבוּעוֹת וְאַרְבָּעָה יָמִים לָעֹמֶר. נצח שבנצח

יא באייר

הַיּוֹם שִׁשָּׁה וְעֶשְׂרִים יוֹם שֶׁהֵם שְׁלֹשָׁה שָׁבוּעוֹת וַחֲמִשָּׁה יָמִים לָעֹמֶר. הוד שבנצח

יב באייר

הַיּוֹם שִׁבְעָה וְעֶשְׂרִים יוֹם שֶׁהֵם שְׁלֹשָׁה שָׁבוּעוֹת וְשִׁשָּׁה יָמִים לָעֹמֶר. יסוד שבנצח

יג באייר

הַיּוֹם שְׁמוֹנָה וְעֶשְׂרִים יוֹם שֶׁהֵם אַרְבָּעָה שָׁבוּעוֹת לָעֹמֶר. מלכות שבנצח

יד באייר, פסח שני

הַיּוֹם תִּשְׁעָה וְעֶשְׂרִים יוֹם שֶׁהֵם אַרְבָּעָה שָׁבוּעוֹת וְיוֹם אֶחָד לָעֹמֶר. חסד שבהוד

טו באייר

הַיּוֹם שְׁלֹשִׁים יוֹם שֶׁהֵם אַרְבָּעָה שָׁבוּעוֹת וּשְׁנֵי יָמִים לָעֹמֶר. גבורה שבהוד

טז באייר

הַיּוֹם אֶחָד וּשְׁלֹשִׁים יוֹם שֶׁהֵם אַרְבָּעָה שָׁבוּעוֹת וּשְׁלֹשָׁה יָמִים לָעֹמֶר. תפארת שבהוד

יז באייר

הַיּוֹם שְׁנַיִם וּשְׁלֹשִׁים יוֹם שֶׁהֵם אַרְבָּעָה שָׁבוּעוֹת וְאַרְבָּעָה יָמִים לָעֹמֶר. נצח שבהוד

יח באייר, ל"ג בעומר

הַיּוֹם שְׁלֹשָׁה וּשְׁלֹשִׁים יוֹם שֶׁהֵם אַרְבָּעָה שָׁבוּעוֹת וַחֲמִשָּׁה יָמִים לָעֹמֶר. הוד שבהוד

יט באייר

הַיּוֹם אַרְבָּעָה וּשְׁלֹשִׁים יוֹם שֶׁהֵם אַרְבָּעָה שָׁבוּעוֹת וְשִׁשָּׁה יָמִים לָעֹמֶר. יסוד שבהוד

כ באייר

הַיּוֹם חֲמִשָּׁה וּשְׁלֹשִׁים יוֹם שֶׁהֵם חֲמִשָּׁה שָׁבוּעוֹת לָעֹמֶר. מלכות שבהוד

כא באייר

הַיּוֹם שִׁשָּׁה וּשְׁלֹשִׁים יוֹם שֶׁהֵם חֲמִשָּׁה שָׁבוּעוֹת וְיוֹם אֶחָד לָעֹמֶר. חסד שביסוד

כב באייר

הַיּוֹם שִׁבְעָה וּשְׁלֹשִׁים יוֹם שֶׁהֵם חֲמִשָּׁה שָׁבוּעוֹת וּשְׁנֵי יָמִים לָעֹמֶר. גבורה שביסוד

כג באייר

הַיּוֹם שְׁמוֹנָה וּשְׁלֹשִׁים יוֹם שֶׁהֵם חֲמִשָּׁה שָׁבוּעוֹת וְשִׁשָּׁה יָמִים לָעֹמֶר. תפארת שביסוד

כד באייר

הַיּוֹם תִּשְׁעָה וּשְׁלֹשִׁים יוֹם שֶׁהֵם חֲמִשָּׁה שָׁבוּעוֹת וְאַרְבָּעָה יָמִים לָעֹמֶר. נצח שביסוד

כה באייר

הַיּוֹם אַרְבָּעִים יוֹם שֶׁהֵם חֲמִשָּׁה שָׁבוּעוֹת וַחֲמִשָּׁה יָמִים לָעֹמֶר. הוד שביסוד

כו באייר

הַיּוֹם אֶחָד וְאַרְבָּעִים יוֹם שֶׁהֵם חֲמִשָּׁה שָׁבוּעוֹת וְשִׁשָּׁה יָמִים לָעֹמֶר. יסוד שביסוד

כז באייר

הַיּוֹם שְׁנַיִם וְאַרְבָּעִים יוֹם שֶׁהֵם שִׁשָּׁה שָׁבוּעוֹת לָעֹמֶר. מלכות שביסוד

כח באייר, יום חרות ירושלים

הַיּוֹם שְׁלֹשָׁה וְאַרְבָּעִים יוֹם שֶׁהֵם שִׁשָּׁה שָׁבוּעוֹת וְיוֹם אֶחָד לָעֹמֶר. חסד שבמלכות

כט באייר

הַיּוֹם אַרְבָּעָה וְאַרְבָּעִים יוֹם שֶׁהֵם שִׁשָּׁה שָׁבוּעוֹת וּשְׁנֵי יָמִים לָעֹמֶר. גבורה שבמלכות

א בסיון, ליל ראש חדש

הַיּוֹם חֲמִשָּׁה וְאַרְבָּעִים יוֹם שֶׁהֵם שִׁשָּׁה שָׁבוּעוֹת וּשְׁלֹשָׁה יָמִים לָעֹמֶר. תפארת שבמלכות

ב' בסיון

הַיּוֹם שִׁשָּׁה וְאַרְבָּעִים יוֹם שֶׁהֵם שִׁשָּׁה שָׁבוּעוֹת וְאַרְבָּעָה יָמִים לָעֹמֶר. נצח שבמלכות

ג' בסיון

הַיּוֹם שִׁבְעָה וְאַרְבָּעִים יוֹם שֶׁהֵם שִׁשָּׁה שָׁבוּעוֹת וַחֲמִשָּׁה יָמִים לָעֹמֶר. הוד שבמלכות

ד' בסיון

הַיּוֹם שְׁמוֹנָה וְאַרְבָּעִים יוֹם שֶׁהֵם שִׁשָּׁה שָׁבוּעוֹת וְשִׁשָּׁה יָמִים לָעֹמֶר. יסוד שבמלכות

ה' בסיון, ערב שבועות

הַיּוֹם תִּשְׁעָה וְאַרְבָּעִים יוֹם שֶׁהֵם שִׁבְעָה שָׁבוּעוֹת לָעֹמֶר. מלכות שבמלכות

הָרַחֲמָן הוּא יַחֲזִיר לָנוּ עֲבוֹדַת בֵּית הַמִּקְדָּשׁ לִמְקוֹמָהּ, בִּמְהֵרָה בְיָמֵינוּ אָמֵן סֶלָה.

לַמְנַצֵּחַ בִּנְגִינוֹת מִזְמוֹר שִׁיר: אֱלֹהִים יְחָנֵּנוּ וִיבָרְכֵנוּ, יָאֵר פָּנָיו אִתָּנוּ, סֶלָה: לָדַעַת בָּאָרֶץ דַּרְכֶּךָ, בְּכָל גּוֹיִם יְשׁוּעָתֶךָ: יוֹדוּךָ עַמִּים אֱלֹהִים, יוֹדוּךָ עַמִּים כֻּלָּם: יִשְׂמְחוּ וִירַנְּנוּ לְאֻמִּים, כִּי תִשְׁפֹּט עַמִּים מִישֹׁר, וּלְאֻמִּים בָּאָרֶץ תַּנְחֵם סֶלָה: יוֹדוּךָ עַמִּים אֱלֹהִים, יוֹדוּךָ עַמִּים כֻּלָּם: אֶרֶץ נָתְנָה יְבוּלָהּ, יְבָרְכֵנוּ אֱלֹהִים אֱלֹהֵינוּ: יְבָרְכֵנוּ אֱלֹהִים, וְיִירְאוּ אוֹתוֹ כָּל אַפְסֵי אָרֶץ:

אָנָּא בְּכֹחַ גְּדֻלַּת יְמִינְךָ תַּתִּיר צְרוּרָה. (אב"ג ית"ץ)

קַבֵּל רִנַּת עַמְּךָ שַׂגְּבֵנוּ טַהֲרֵנוּ נוֹרָא. (קר"ע שט"ן)

נָא גִבּוֹר דּוֹרְשֵׁי יִחוּדְךָ כְּבָבַת שָׁמְרֵם. (נג"ד יכ"ש)

בָּרְכֵם טַהֲרֵם רַחֲמֵם צִדְקָתְךָ תָּמִיד גָּמְלֵם. (בט"ר צת"ג)

חֲסִין קָדוֹשׁ בְּרֹב טוּבְךָ נַהֵל עֲדָתֶךָ. (חק"ב טנ"ע)

יָחִיד גֵּאֶה לְעַמְּךָ פְּנֵה זוֹכְרֵי קְדֻשָּׁתֶךָ. (יג"ל פז"ק)

שַׁוְעָתֵנוּ קַבֵּל וּשְׁמַע צַעֲקָתֵנוּ יוֹדֵעַ תַּעֲלֻמוֹת. (שק"ו צי"ת)

בָּרוּךְ שֵׁם כְּבוֹד מַלְכוּתוֹ לְעוֹלָם וָעֶד.

Haruki Murakami

After Dark

TRANSLATED
FROM THE JAPANESE
BY

Jay Rubin

Harvill
Secker
LONDON

Published by Harvill Secker, 2007

2 4 6 8 10 9 7 5 3 1

Copyright © Haruki Murakami, 2004

English translation copyright © Jay Rubin, 2007

Haruki Murakami has asserted his right under the Copyright, Designs and Patents
Act 1988 to be identified as the author of this work

First published with the title *Afutādāku*
by Kodansha, Tokyo, 2004

First published in Great Britain in 2007 by
HARVILL SECKER, Random House
20 Vauxhall Bridge Road
London SW1V 2SA

www.randomhouse.co.uk

Addresses for companies within The Random House Group Limited can be found
at: www.randomhouse.co.uk/offices.htm

The Random House Group Limited Reg. No. 954009

A CIP catalogue record for this book is available from the British Library

ISBN 9781846550478 (hardback)
ISBN 9781846550485 (trade paperback)

The Random House Group Limited makes every effort to ensure that the papers
used in its books are made from trees that have been legally sourced from
well-managed and credibly certified forests. Our paper procurement policy
can be found at: www.randomhouse.co.uk/paper.htm

Printed and bound in Great Britain by
Clays Ltd, St Ives plc

After Dark

p.m.

1

Eyes mark the shape of the city.

Through the eyes of a high-flying night bird, we take in the scene from midair. In our broad sweep, the city looks like a single gigantic creature—or more like a single collective entity created by many intertwining organisms. Countless arteries stretch to the ends of its elusive body, circulating a continuous supply of fresh blood cells, sending out new data and collecting the old, sending out new consumables and collecting the old, sending out new contradictions and collecting the old. To the rhythm of its pulsing, all parts of the body flicker and flare up and squirm. Midnight is approaching, and while the peak of activity has passed, the basal metabolism that maintains life continues undiminished, producing the basso continuo of the city's moan, a monotonous sound that neither rises nor falls but is pregnant with foreboding.

Our line of sight chooses an area of concentrated brightness and, focusing there, silently descends to it—a sea of neon colours. They call this place an "amusement district." The giant digital screens fastened to the sides of buildings fall silent as midnight approaches, but loud-speakers on storefronts keep pumping out exaggerated hip-hop bass lines. A large game centre crammed with young people; wild electronic sounds; a group of college students spilling out from a bar; teenage girls with brilliant bleached hair, healthy legs thrusting out from microminiskirts; dark-suited men racing across diagonal crossings for the last trains to the suburbs. Even at this hour, the karaoke club pitchmen keep shouting for customers. A flashy black station wagon drifts down the street as if taking stock of the district through its black-tinted windows. The car looks like a deep-sea creature with specialised skin and organs. Two young policemen patrol the street with tense expressions, but no one seems to notice them. The district plays by its own rules at a time like this. The season is late autumn. No wind is blowing, but the air carries a chill. The date is just about to change.

We are inside a Denny's.

Unremarkable but adequate lighting; expressionless decor and tableware; floor plan designed to the last detail by management engineers; innocuous background music at low volume; staff meticulously trained to deal with customers by the book: "Welcome to Denny's." Everything about the restaurant is anonymous and interchangeable. And almost every seat is filled.

After a quick survey of the interior, our eyes come to rest on a girl sitting by the front window. Why her? Why not someone else? Hard to say. But, for some reason, she attracts our attention—very naturally. She sits at a four-person table, reading a book. Hooded grey parka, blue jeans, yellow sneakers faded from repeated washing. On the back of the chair next to her hangs a varsity jacket. This, too, is far from new. She is probably college freshman age, though an air of high school still clings to her. Hair black, short, and straight. Little make-up, no jewellery. Small, slender face. Black-rimmed glasses. Every now and then, an earnest wrinkle forms between her brows.

She reads with great concentration. Her eyes rarely move from the pages of her book—a thick hardback. A bookstore wrapper hides the title from us. Judging from her intent expression, the book might contain challenging subject matter. Far from skimming, she seems to be biting off and chewing it one line at a time.

On her table is a coffee cup. And an ashtray. Next to the ashtray, a navy blue baseball cap with a Boston Red Sox "B." It might be a little too large for her head. A brown leather shoulder bag rests on the seat next to her. It bulges as if its contents had been thrown in on the spur of the moment. She reaches out at regular intervals and brings the coffee cup to her mouth, but she doesn't appear to be enjoying the flavour. She drinks because she has a cup of coffee in front of her: that is her role as a customer. At odd moments, she puts a cigarette between her lips and lights it with a plastic lighter. She narrows her eyes, releases an easy puff of smoke into the air, puts the cigarette into the ashtray, and then, as if to soothe an approaching headache, she strokes her temples with her fingertips.

The music playing at low volume is "Go Away Little Girl" by Percy Faith and his Orchestra. No one is listening, of course. Many different kinds of people are taking meals and drinking coffee in this late-night Denny's, but she is the only female there alone. She raises her face from her book now and then to glance at her watch, but she seems dissatisfied with the slow passage of time. Not that she appears to be waiting for anyone: she doesn't look around the restaurant or train her eyes on the front door. She just keeps reading her book, lighting an occasional cigarette, mechanically tipping back her coffee cup, and hoping for the time to pass a little faster. Needless to say, dawn will not be here for hours.

She breaks off her reading and looks outside. From this second-storey window she can look down on the busy street. Even at a time like this, the street is bright enough and filled with people coming and going—people with places to go and people with no place to go; people with a purpose and people with no purpose; people trying to hold time back and people trying to urge it forward. After a long, steady look at this jumbled street scene, she holds her breath for a moment and turns her eyes once again towards her book. She reaches for her coffee cup. Puffed no more than two or three times, her cigarette turns into a perfectly formed column of ash in the ashtray.

The electric door slides open and a lanky young man walks in. Short black leather coat, wrinkled olive-green chinos, brown work boots. Hair fairly long and tangled in places. Perhaps he has had no chance to wash it in some days. Perhaps he has just crawled out of the underbrush somewhere. Or perhaps he just finds it more natural and comfortable to have messy hair. His thinness makes him look less elegant than malnourished. A big black instrument case hangs from his shoulder. Wind instrument. He also holds a dirty tote bag at his side. It seems to be stuffed with sheet music and other assorted things. His right cheek bears an eye-catching scar. It is short and deep, as if the flesh has been gouged out by something sharp. Nothing else about him stands out. He is a very ordinary young man with the air of a nice—but not very clever—stray mutt.

The waitress on hostess duty shows him to a seat at the back of the restaurant. He passes the table of the girl with the book. A few steps beyond it, he comes to a halt as if a thought has struck him. He begins moving slowly backwards as in a rewinding film, stopping at her table. He cocks his head and studies her face. He is trying to remember something, and much time goes by until he gets it. He seems like the type for whom everything takes time.

The girl senses his presence and raises her face from her book. She narrows her eyes and looks at the young man standing there. He is so tall, she seems to be looking far overhead. Their eyes meet. The young man smiles. His smile is meant to show he means no harm.

"Sorry if I've got the wrong person," he says, "but aren't you Eri Asai's little sister?"

She does not answer. She looks at him with eyes that could be looking at an overgrown bush in the corner of a garden.

"We met once," he continues. "Your name is . . . Yuri . . . sort of like your sister Eri's except the first syllable."

Keeping a cautious gaze fixed on him, she executes a concise factual correction: "Mari."

He raises his index finger and says, "That's it! Mari. Eri and Mari. Different first syllables. You don't remember me, do you?"

Mari inclines her head slightly. This could mean either yes or no. She takes off her glasses and sets them down beside her coffee cup.

The waitress retraces her steps and asks, "Are you together?"

"Uh-huh," he answers. "We are."

She sets his menu on the table. He takes the seat across from Mari and puts his case on the seat next to his. A moment later he thinks to ask Mari, "Mind if I sit here a while? I'll get out as soon as I'm finished eating. I have to meet somebody."

Mari gives him a slight frown. "Aren't you supposed to say that *before* you sit down?"

He thinks about the meaning of her words. "That I have to meet somebody?"

"No . . ." Mari says.

"Oh, you mean as a matter of politeness."

"Uh-huh."

He nods. "You're right. I should have asked if it's okay to sit at your table. I'm sorry. But the place is crowded, and I won't bother you for long. Do you mind?"

Mari gives her shoulders a little shrug that seems to mean "As you wish." He opens his menu and studies it.

"Are you through eating?" he asks.

"I'm not hungry."

With a scowl, he scans the menu, snaps it shut, and lays it on the table. "I really don't have to open the menu," he says. "I'm just faking it."

Mari doesn't say anything.

"I don't eat anything but chicken salad here. Ever. If you ask me, the only thing worth eating at Denny's is the chicken salad. I've had just about everything on the menu. Have you ever tried their chicken salad?"

Mari shakes her head.

"It's not bad. Chicken salad and crispy toast. That's all I ever eat at Denny's."

"So why do you even bother looking at the menu?"

He pulls at the wrinkles in the corner of one eye with his little finger. "Just think about it. Wouldn't it be too sad to walk into Denny's and order chicken salad without looking at the menu? It's like telling the world, 'I come to Denny's all the time because I love the chicken salad.' So I always go through the motion of opening the menu and pretending I picked the chicken salad after considering other things."

The waitress brings him water and he orders chicken

salad and crispy toast. "Make it really crispy," he says with conviction. "Almost burnt." He also orders coffee for afterwards. The waitress inputs his order using a hand-held device and confirms it by reading it aloud.

"And I think the young lady needs a refill," he says, pointing at Mari's cup.

"Thank you, sir. I will bring the coffee right away."

He watches her go off.

"You don't like chicken?" he asks.

"It's not that," Mari says. "But I make a point of not eating chicken out."

"Why not?"

"Especially the chicken they serve in chain restaurants —they're full of weird drugs. Growth hormones and stuff. The chickens are locked in these dark, narrow cages, and given all these shots, and their feed is full of chemicals, and they're put on conveyor belts, and machines cut their heads off and pluck them . . ."

"Whoa!" he says with a smile. The wrinkles at the corners of his eyes deepen. "Chicken salad à la George Orwell!"

Mari narrows her eyes and looks at him. She can't tell if he is making fun of her.

"Anyhow," he says, "the chicken salad here is not bad. Really."

As if suddenly recalling that he is wearing it, he takes off his leather coat, folds it, and lays it on the seat next to his. Then he rubs his hands together atop the table. He has on a green, coarse-knit crew-neck sweater. Like his hair, the wool of the sweater is tangled in places. He is obviously not the sort who pays a lot of attention to his appearance.

"We met at a hotel swimming pool in Shinagawa. Two summers ago. Remember?"

"Sort of."

"My buddy was there, your sister was there, you were there, and I was there. Four of us all together. We had just entered college, and I'm pretty sure you were in your second year of high school. Right?"

Mari nods without much apparent interest.

"My friend was kinda dating your sister then. He brought me along on like a double date. He dug up four free tickets to the pool, and your sister brought you along. You hardly said a word, though. You spent the whole time in the pool, swimming like a young dolphin. We went to the hotel tea room for ice cream afterwards. You ordered a peach melba."

Mari frowns. "How come you remember stuff like that?"

"I never dated a girl who ate peach melba before. And you were cute, of course."

Mari looks at him blankly. "Liar. You were staring at my sister the whole time."

"I was?"

Mari answers with silence.

"Maybe I was," he says. "For some reason I remember her bikini was really tiny."

Mari pulls out a cigarette, puts it between her lips, and lights it with her lighter.

"Let me tell you something," he says. "I'm not trying to

defend Denny's or anything, but I'm pretty sure that smoking a whole pack of cigarettes is *way* worse for you than eating a plate of chicken salad that *might* have some problems with it. Don't you think so?"

Mari ignores his question.

"Another girl was supposed to go with my sister that time, but she got sick at the last minute and my sister forced me to go with her. To keep the numbers right."

"So you were in a bad mood."

"I remember you, though."

"Really?"

Mari puts her finger on her right cheek.

The young man touches the deep scar on his own cheek. "Oh, this. When I was a kid, I was going too fast on my bike and couldn't make the turn at the bottom of the hill. Another inch and I would have lost my right eye. My earlobe's deformed, too. Wanna see it?"

Mari frowns and shakes her head.

The waitress brings the chicken salad and toast to the table. She pours fresh coffee into Mari's cup and checks to make sure she has brought all the ordered items to the table. He picks up his knife and fork and, with practised movements, begins eating his chicken salad. Then he picks up a piece of toast, stares at it, and wrinkles his brow.

"No matter how much I scream at them to make my toast as crispy as possible, I have never once got it the way I want it. I can't imagine why. What with Japanese industriousness and high-tech culture and the market principles that the Denny's chain is always pursuing, it shouldn't be that hard to get crispy toast, don't you think? So, why can't they do it? Of what value is a civilisation that can't toast a piece of bread as ordered?"

Mari doesn't take him up on this.

"But anyhow, your sister was a real beauty," the young man says, as if talking to himself.

Mari looks up. "Why do you say that in the past tense?"

"Why do I . . . ? I mean, I'm talking about something that happened a long time ago, so I used the past tense, that's all. I'm not saying she isn't a beauty now or anything."

"She's still pretty, I think."

"Well, that's just dandy. But, to tell you the truth, I don't know Eri Asai all that well. We were in the same class for a year in high school, but I hardly said two words to her. It might be more accurate to say she wouldn't give me the time of day."

"You're still interested in her, right?"

The young man stops his knife and fork in midair and thinks for a moment. "Interested. Hmm. Maybe as a kind of intellectual curiosity."

"Intellectual curiosity?"

"Yeah, like, what would it feel like to go out on a date with a beautiful girl like Eri Asai? I mean, she's an absolute cover girl."

"You call that *intellectual* curiosity?"

"Kind of, yeah."

"But back then, your friend was the one going out with her, and you were the other guy on a double date."

13

He nods with a mouthful of food, which he then takes all the time he needs to chew.

"I'm kind of a low-key guy. The spotlight doesn't suit me. I'm more of a side dish—coleslaw or French fries or a Wham! back-up singer."

"Which is why you were paired with me."

"But still, you were pretty damn cute."

"Is there something about your personality that makes you prefer the past tense?"

The young man smiles. "No, I was just directly expressing how I felt back then from the perspective of the present. You were very cute. Really. You hardly talked to me, though."

He rests his knife and fork on his plate, takes a drink of water, and wipes his mouth with a paper napkin. "So, while you were swimming, I asked Eri Asai, 'Why won't your little sister talk to me? Is there something wrong with me?' "

"What'd she say?"

"That you never take the initiative to talk to anybody. That you're kinda different, and that even though you're Japanese you speak more often in Chinese than Japanese. So I shouldn't worry. She didn't think there was anything especially wrong with me."

Mari silently crushes her cigarette out in the ashtray.

"It's true, isn't it? There wasn't anything especially wrong with me, was there?"

Mari thinks for a moment. "I don't remember all that well, but I don't think there was anything wrong with you."

"That's good. I was worried. Of course, I *do* have a few things wrong with me, but those are strictly problems I keep inside. I'd hate to think they were obvious to anybody else. Especially at a swimming pool in the summer."

Mari looks at him again as if to confirm the accuracy of his statement. "I don't think I was aware of any problems you had inside."

"That's a relief."

"I can't remember your name, though," Mari says.

"My name?"

"Your name."

He shakes his head. "I don't mind if you forgot my name. It's about as ordinary as a name can be. Even I feel like forgetting it sometimes. It's not that easy, though, to forget your own name. Other people's names—even ones I have to remember—I'm always forgetting."

He glances out of the window as if in search of something he should not have lost. Then he turns towards Mari again.

"One thing always mystified me, and that is, why didn't your sister ever get into the pool that time? It was a hot day, and a really nice pool."

Mari looks at him as if to say, *You mean you don't get that, either?* "She didn't want her make-up to wash off. It's so obvious. And you can't really swim in a bathing suit like that."

"Is that it?" he says. "It's amazing how two sisters can be so different."

"We live two different lives."

He thinks about her words for a few moments and then says, "I wonder how it turns out that we all lead such different lives. Take you and your sister, for example. You're born to the same parents, you grow up in the same household, you're both girls. How do you end up with such wildly different personalities? At what point do you, like, go your separate ways? One puts on a bikini like little semaphore flags and lies by the pool looking sexy, and the other puts on her school bathing suit and swims her heart out like a dolphin . . ."

Mari looks at him. "Are you asking me to explain it to you here and now in twenty-five words or less while you eat your chicken salad?"

He shakes his head. "No, I was just saying what popped into my head out of curiosity or something. You don't have to answer. I was just asking myself."

He starts to work on his chicken salad again, changes his mind, and continues:

"I don't have any brothers or sisters, so I just wanted to know: up to what point do they resemble each other, and where do their differences come in?"

Mari remains silent while the young man with the knife and fork in his hands stares thoughtfully at a point in space above the table.

Then he says, "I once read a story about three brothers who washed up on an island in Hawaii. A myth. An old one. I read it when I was a kid, so I probably don't have the story exactly right, but it goes something like this. Three brothers went out fishing and got caught in a storm. They drifted on the ocean for a long time until